General Barillas, President of Guatemala.

IN AND OUT OF
CENTRAL AMERICA

AND OTHER SKETCHES
AND STUDIES OF TRAVEL

BY

FRANK VINCENT

AUTHOR OF "ACTUAL AFRICA," "AROUND AND ABOUT SOUTH AMERICA"
"NORSK, LAPP, AND FINN," ETC.

WITH MAPS AND ILLUSTRATIONS

FOURTH EDITION

NEW YORK
D. APPLETON AND COMPANY
1896

CONTENTS.

ILLUSTRATIONS.

MAPS.

CENTRAL AMERICA

Mr. Vincent's Route

SCALE OF STATUTE MILES

0   25   50   100   150   200

MEXICO

GUATEMALA

VERA PAZ

TOTONICAPAN

Ciudad Real

Usumasinta R.

Lake Peten

Dolores

Cohan

BRITISH HONDURAS

BELIZE

TURNEFFE I.

G. of Honduras

Rio Hondo

QUEZALT.

Totonicapan
Quezaltenango
Enango
Sololá
La Tesulla
Antigua
Fuego (Vol.)

Po. San José

Champerico

Mazatlan

SONSONATE
Sonsonate
Acajutla

SAN SALVADOR
Po. Libertad
S. SALV.

Santa Ana
Sta. Ana
San Vicente
S. Miguel

Sacatecoluca

SAN MIGUEL

FONSECA BAY

La Union
Amapala

Chinandega
Corinto

Mombacho (Vol.)

MANAGUA

Momotombo (Vol.)

GRANADA

Rivas or Nicaragua

S. Juan del Sur

C. Blanco

G. OF NICOYA

SAN JOSÉ

Punta Arenas

Cartago
Irazu (Vol.)

C. Matapalo

Pt. Mariato

MOSQUITO GULF

Chiriqui Bay
C. Valientes

Pt. Burica

BAY OF PANAMA

Aspinwall
Panama

HONDURAS

COMAYAGUA
Comayagua

TEGUCIGALPA
Tegucigalpa

Santa Barbara

Gracias

Choluteca

OLANCHO

YORO
Yoro

C. Honduras

BAY IS.

SEGOVIA

Matagalpa

NICARAGUA
Managua

LAKE NICARAGUA

San Juan del Norte
(Greytown)

Bluefields

MOSQUITO RESERVATION

Pearl Cays Pt.

ST. ANDREW I.

OLD PROVIDENCE I.

MOSQUITO CAYS

C. Gracias a Dios

VIVORILLA CAYS

Patuca R.

Wanks R.

Segovia R.

RONCADO I.

GORDO CAYS

COLOMBIA

PANAMA

CARIBBEAN SEA

PACIFIC OCEAN

Longitude   West from   Greenwich

18   16   14   12   10   8

93   91   89   87   85   83   81

I.

IN AND OUT OF CENTRAL AMERICA.

INTRODUCTORY.

THERE are many lines of steamers by which Central America may be reached from the United States, though some of the routes are roundabout and tedious. To say nothing of several lines of fruiting steamers which go from New York and from New Orleans to various ports on the Caribbean (the Atlantic) coast, we have, of course, the comfortable large steamers of the Pacific Mail Company, which sail three times a month from New York to Aspinwall, and connect, *via* the Panama Railroad, with others that go from Panama to San Francisco. These call at about one half of the Pacific Central American ports, while three other steamers of the same line touch each month at all of them. A Spanish line has two steamers per month from Panama to San Francisco, calling at all ports. An American company sends one steamer a month from Guatemala to San Francisco, touching at ports all along the coasts of Mexico and Lower California; and a Mexican steamer runs once a month from Guatemala to Guaymas, in the Gulf of California, whence the Mexican Sonora Railway connects, by a road three hundred and fifty miles long, with our Southern Pacific and Atchison, Topeka and Santa Fé Railroads. The steamers, therefore, are numerous enough, but they carry you such winding ways that while by the shortest route it would take at least ten days to reach a capital of one of the republics, by the longest you would need one whole month.

First, let me correct some popular impressions about Central America as to size and population. Its entire area is a little less than that of our State of California, or, including Balize (the colony of British Honduras, which may very properly be reckoned with it), its area is a little less than that of France, while its total population is but that of the city of Paris! Of course it lies wholly within the tropics, though it is the belts adjoining each ocean which have torrid climates. The high lands of the interior, five and six thousand feet above the sea, could have been no more effectively situated in a temperate zone. Central America extends in a general northwest and southeast direction, between ten degrees each of latitude and longitude (namely, the parallels of 8° and 18° north and 82° and 92° west), a total length of nearly one thousand miles; while the greatest breadth, that along the northern boundary of Nicaragua, is but three hundred miles, and the least, in Costa Rica, not one hundred. In fact, in the central axis of Costa Rica stands a not very conspicuous mountain, from whose summit, in clear weather, both oceans may easily be seen. Nicaragua and Costa Rica have nearly as much sea-coast upon one ocean as upon the other. Honduras has by far the greater portion on the Atlantic, and Guatemala on the Pacific, each having but one good seaport on its lesser extent of coast. Salvador looks only upon the Pacific, and Balize upon the Atlantic. In fact, Balize stands in about the same relation, in size and shape, to Guatemala as does Salvador to Honduras, remembering, of course, that they are upon opposite sides of the vast isthmus.

The usually accurate Humboldt mistakes in saying that the chain of the Andes extends unbroken from Colombia to Mexico. There are a great many short irregular ranges, and their general trend is east and west. Honduras is so broken and hillocky as to have reminded me of the West India island of Dominica, whose surface Columbus aptly compared to the appearance of a lot of stiff paper after being rumpled in the hand. The volcanoes—of which there are some fifty in Central America, most of them being extinct—though more or less isolated, appear to be in irregular lines not far distant from the Pacific. The general superficial appearance of Central America may be said to be—save on the Caribbean coasts, where it is low and level—that of a region of forest-clad hills, fertile valleys, large lakes, and small rivers. All the capitals are in the interior, and are situated generally at an altitude of from three to five thousand feet, where the climate is cool and salubrious; the seaports connecting with the capitals are small, hot, and unhealthy.

The history of Central America is perhaps too well known to necessitate more than a reference to the fact that the five republics now found there formed originally a colony or province of Spain (called, by the way, Guatemala), under the viceroyalty of a captain-general. In 1823 they established their independence, and constituted a federation styled the " United States of Central America," with a President and a Federal Congress modeled upon our own. This union lasted only sixteen years, when the different members of the confederation became sovereign and independent. Several attempts have since been made to unite these republics—that of Barrios being fresh in the minds of all. The states of Central America are no less active in revolution and in warring with each other than those of South America. However, in February, 1889, the Central American republics agreed upon a treaty, which it is hoped will help to bring about a lasting union. It provides that if any difficulty shall arise between these states, it shall be settled without war by the arbitration of some one of the following nations: the United States, Argentine Republic, Chili, Mexico, Switzerland, or of any of the great European powers; that none of the five republics shall form alliances with outside nations without the consent of all; and that delegates from the five republics shall meet annually to consider matters of mutual interest.

Naturally it is impossible to travel to advantage in Central America without a thorough knowledge of the Spanish language. Through the help of foreign residents you may possibly succeed in getting to the capitals, but such a visit will lose half its flavor and value. The sole dependence for interior travel is the mule. The roads are generally mere trails, and all but impassable during the rainy season—nearly one half the year. There are less than four hundred miles of railway in all Central America, and trains are generally run at about the speed of ordinary glaciers. Hence, though Costa Rica has more than one hundred miles of railway, the mail is carried on mule-back, while in parts of Salvador and Honduras it is actually borne afoot. The train that pierces the most populous districts of Costa Rica until quite recently ran only when there were sufficient freight and passengers to "pay," and even now its trips are but tri-weekly. There are several fair cart-roads, but you seldom find lines of stages running upon them. Such conveniences as "through routes" are non-existent. No train was ever known to connect with a steamer, no stage with a train, scarcely any mule with a stage. Your only dependence, as I have just said, is upon the stout and patient mule—a generally, though wrongfully, abused animal which has carried me safely for many thousands of miles. When about to undertake a journey, you must engage mules not only for yourself, baggage, and servant, but often for tents and provisions also. The hotels in the seaports are mere sheds or warehouses, dirty, full of fleas, mosquitoes, and, even worse, with wretched food, badly cooked. In some of the capitals approximations to comfortable hotels are found; but they are pretty sure to be managed by foreigners—either Frenchmen, Italians, or Germans. Travel is generally undertaken at night, to avoid the heat and glare of day, and twelve hours at a stretch in the saddle are not thought an excessive ride. The traveler, therefore, who sees very much of the interior may expect to encounter many petty inconveniences, annoyances, and hardships. Though peril is not always added, yet it will be well to wear conspicuously a revolver, since its possessor will thus receive proper attention and be free from insult—not that there will probably be any actual necessity for its use. For traveling expenses, United States gold coin may be taken, or Chilian and Peruvian silver dollars, the latter being the more bulky, but freely circulating at their full value in all the republics. Several of these have paper money also, which, though easier to carry, is usually so much depreciated in value that the country people are suspicious of it. No passport to enter is at present required, though sometimes permits to leave, as in Guatemala and Costa Rica, are necessary.

Among the 2,500,000 inhabitants of Central America you find, besides pure Indians and negroes, a great number of curiously crossed races. A Spaniard is here, of course, as much of a foreigner as a Japanese would be. Perhaps a quarter of the population are creoles, or people of European parentage. Among the mixed races you notice especially the mestizoes, or descendants of a white father and Indian mother; mulattoes, the offspring of whites and Africans; and the zamboes, half-breed negroes and Indians. All tints are to be seen, from the chalky white of the hill-dwellers of Costa Rica—the purest native blood—shading almost imperceptibly down, through octoroons and quadroons, to reddish-colored Indians and, finally, coal-black negroes. Negroes are found in any number only on the Caribbean side and chiefly in the British province of Balize. In Guatemala are a great many Indians—aborigines, or their direct descendants. You notice them especially in the streets and markets of the capital, and they always prove interesting. They belong to the great Quiché family, of which as many as fifty tribes are scattered through Central America. In Guatemala there are sixteen aboriginal idioms. About one thousand foreigners—Germans, English, French, Italians, and Americans—live there. The members of the diplomatic corps accredited to the five states make their headquarters in Guatemala, going, as business may require, to the other capitals. They all have the rank of minister-resident. Only seven foreign powers are at present represented—England, France, Spain, Austria, Germany, Italy, and the United States. In each of the other republics a few foreigners reside on their coffee or sugar estates, or engage in mercantile affairs.

The real wealth of Central America is in its vegetable productions, though minerals are fast becoming an important industry. In Honduras and Salvador several (North) American mining companies do business. Honduras is altogether the richest country in mineral resources, gold, silver, copper, zinc, lead, platina, quicksilver, iron, coal, opals, asbestos, and marble having been found there. At present, gold and silver are about the only ores mined. The chief export of Central America is coffee, and next in order would probably follow cabinet woods and dye woods, gold and silver bullion, sugar, and fruits. The greater part of the export trade is with Great Britain and the United States, while the imports are chiefly from Germany, France, and Great Britain. In addition to the duties on imports and exports, the revenues are largely derived from monopolies of spirits and tobacco. These countries have, too, the same simple and high-principled manner of getting rid of their just debts, or large portions of them, as have Turkey, Spain, and Peru. Sometimes the process is known as " consolidating," again as " converting," rarely as " refunding," most often as " scaling." The method might at least with great propriety be designated as very " scaly." Aggregates are reduced from fifty to seventy-five per cent merely by a stroke of the pen and a notice in the official gazette. Honduras, altogether the poorest and most backward of these republics, has the large debt of $31,000,-000, interest mostly unpaid. Nicaragua and Salvador have relatively small debts, but both these states are poor and inert. It can not be that any of the Central American republics are, like the effete monarchies of Europe, impoverished by their war establishments, for the sum total of their armies gives but six thousand men, and navies there are none. An ordinary revolution in these countries—such as occurs every few months — will not have engaged on both sides more than one hundred men, and you generally notice among the lists of killed and wounded about as many major-generals as high-privates.

The government of each of these republics is vested in a president, who is generally elected for four years, one or two vice-presidents, and four or six ministers. The legislative power is intrusted to a congress of senators and deputies. Suffrage is universal. The Roman Catholic is, of course, the state religion, and is generally duly recognized as such, though other religions are protected. In Guatemala, however, the clerical government was overthrown in 1871, and many of the old convents and churches have been turned into Government offices, schools, and hotels. Thus, in the capital, the Bureau of Liquors and Tobacco now occupies the building where once the Dominican Friars held undisputed sway. The Revenue and Customs Bureau occupies the Franciscan convent, and the Post-Office is in the building which once sheltered the members of the First Order of St. Francis. The Government Palace was once church property. The Grand Hotel was formerly the private residence of a wealthy Catholic family who, for using the Church power politically, were banished by Barrios, and had their property confiscated. Education, though not general in Central America, is yet becoming prominent in at least two of the states—Guatemala and Salvador. Guatemala has naturally the largest number of educational institutions, and their general excellence and cheapness serve to draw pupils from the other and smaller republics. Besides

2

those of the varying grades and the professional schools (military, engineering, medical, etc.), evening schools are provided for mechanics and workingmen, and special schools are opened for girls.

By the way, Salvador, and not San Salvador (as we were taught at school), is the official title of the smallest of the five republics. San Salvador is the name of the capital. Salvador has a great number of volcanoes, and so has Nicaragua. One day, at Leon, the largest city in Nicaragua, I counted fourteen volcanoes in sight from the cathedral roof. Several of these are continuously active, their steep and smooth purple cones, with spirals of fleecy smoke curling lazily upward, giving always a unique and pleasing character to the landscape. But just at present Nicaragua is chiefly interesting from its proposed interoceanic canal, while Salvador provokes most attention because of its frequent and severe earthquake shocks. Guatemala, however, is the most prosperous and important, contains more than half the population of all Central America, and has a revenue greater than that of all the other republics combined. Its capital has upward of sixty thousand inhabitants, and is a sort of miniature city of Mexico—as Brussels is a diminutive Paris—in fact, its citizens are very fond of styling it the " Paris of Central America." There you find paved and clean streets, the electric light, horse cars, telephones, fine Government buildings, a large and imposing opera-house, pretty parks, good hackney carriages, and you observe that the city is admirably policed by men wearing the

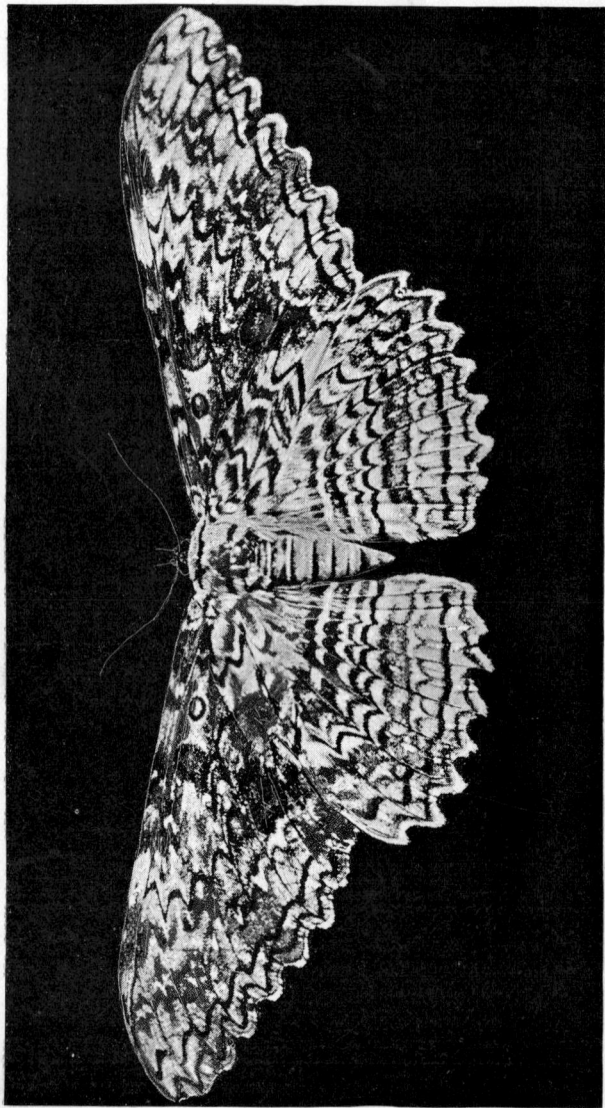

A Moth Eleven Inches from Tip to Tip of Wing.

identical uniform of the New York "guardians of the peace." There are daily newspapers, clubs, and, near at hand, open-air swimming baths and a race-course. In short, in both capital and country, Guatemala is especially interesting.

Having now given a somewhat general and hasty view of Central America, I shall next proceed in detail to the narrative of my visit to its five little republics.

1. COSTA RICA.

In September, 1887, I left New York in the Pacific Mail steamer Newport for Aspinwall, where, after a remarkably pleasant voyage of nine days, I safely arrived, crossing the Isthmus of Panama the same day. Two days afterward I sailed in the steamer Clyde, of the Central American and Mexican Line, for Punta Arenas, the Pacific seaport of Costa Rica, four hundred and fifty-four miles distant. On the morning of October 2d we passed the peninsula of Burica, one half of which belongs to Costa Rica and the other to the Republic of Colombia the boundary line between South and Central America running hence in a northeasterly direction to the Caribbean Sea. Next we crossed the mouth of the Gulf of Dolce, from which a canal route to the Chiriqui Lagoon was once surveyed. The coast of Costa Rica from here to the Gulf of Nicoya is hilly, descending generally abruptly to the ocean, and densely covered with forest. As we neared Punta Arenas great patches of grassland, here and there, were visible. No evidence of human habitation was apparent until we entered the gulf, which is a great expanse of water with ample depth for the largest vessels. Its shores are quite diversified with little wooded islands and cone-shaped hills, though none of the latter reach a greater altitude than two thousand feet. But little of the town of Punta Arenas appears from the Gulf of Nicoya. A long way off you see an iron wharf, covered with a great iron-roofed building, and back of it the two or three houses of the Customs Department and Post-Office. The gently sloping beach is very broad and smooth, and of dark, almost black, sand. On either side are immense stretches of cocoanut-palms. Beyond the town rise cloud-capped, forest-clad hills, extending north and south. No vessels of any sort were in port, though a few lighters were anchored near the wharf. There were no lighthouses, but an old locomotive headlight, on the end of the wharf, served the necessary purpose. Only two passengers were bound for Costa Rica—my traveling companion, a Brazilian by birth and parentage and an American by choice and naturalization, and myself. After a visit from the port and custom officers, we took boat for the shore. From one building floated the flag of Costa Rica, an oblong banner with vertical stripes— two of blue, two of white, and one of red in the center, representing the five provinces of the republic. As we neared the wharf, I noticed a railway car at the edge

of the jungle, to the right, and upon a lighter just
before us, a dozen great uncouth pelicans sitting in a
row. At the end of the wharf was a steam-crane,
which is used to raise freight from the lighters, and
also passengers when the sea is very rough, as it frequently is. The machinery stood on a foundation that
made a complete circuit, thus loading directly into
hand-cars which ran through the custom-house building
to the railroad that extends a portion of the way toward
the capital of San José. The custom-house examination
was long, minute and exasperating, nearly everything being taken from our trunks and every small package being
opened. Duties are high, and there is besides a wharfage
for every pound of baggage or freight received upon the
pier. No other landing is in use. The town takes its
name, Punta Arenas, from the sandy point or peninsula
upon which it is built, a low, narrow, and level expanse
of sand, which extends a long distance into the gulf.
Near its eastern juncture with the mainland a large river
enters the gulf, thus making a protected harbor, though
one of not very deep water. The town is laid out at right
angles, with wide streets, along the centers of which at
frequent intervals extend posts supporting kerosene lamps.
The sidewalks are narrow and formed of rough stones,
and sometimes of bricks or tiles. The streets are much
overgrown with grass. Orange, lime, and magnolia trees
shade the sidewalks, and cocoanut-palms, papayas, tama-
rinds, mangoes, bananas, and almonds—their foliage growing in horizontal strata—abound in the gardens. The

dwellings are half concealed by these trees and by flowers, besides having large orchards of fruit trees adjoining. In this way you do not realize the size of the town until after a walk over it, though its population may not be more than five thousand. A popular style of fence is formed of growing cacti eight feet or more in height. The dwellings are usually of but one story, with boarded sides and a tiled roof. The solitary hotel of the place is also in this style, while its partitions reach only to a point that is on a level with the eaves. This gives more air but less privacy. Meals, at which beans, rice, and bananas always figure, are given at 10 A. M. and 4 P. M. These are equivalent to two full dinners per day, and in addition coffee and bread and butter are served from 6 to 8 A. M. In this climate the windows are glassless and all the houses have piazzas. Hammocks or canvas cots are used for sleeping purposes. The stores contain multifarious stocks. There are many drinking shops, where the native rum—*aguardiente*—and imported beers are retailed. The market consists of a large quadrangle of sheds, with limited varieties of produce exposed for sale. The poorer class of dwellings are mere huts, with bamboo sides and grass roofs. The natives are of a light-brown, mahogany color, of good height, and well formed. They are mestizoes, or crosses between whites and Indians of varying strains. All bear amiable, smiling faces. The men have very scant beard but generally heavy shocks of hair, while the women have very long and thick black, glossy hair which they generally wear braided and coiled upon the back of the head or in two long braids hanging down the back. The men content themselves with straw hat and calico shirt and trousers, or more often merely a merino undershirt in place of the cotton shirt. The women wear very low-cut chemises and gay-colored skirts, and, loosely placed upon the shoulders or sometimes lifted upon the head, a light shawl or mantilla of some dark color. Most of the men and women go barefooted. The women have the attractive habit of wearing flowers in their hair, a small bouquet being often secured with a large tortoise-shell comb in a very piquant fashion. The men do not seem to be such inveterate smokers as those of the South American states, but, curiously enough, the women are rarely seen without cigarette or cigar.

Though Punta Arenas is the largest seaport of Costa Rica and on the direct road to the capital, I was not, on this account, the less sure of finding a primitive condition of affairs. One of the first indications of this was that there was but one mail a day to the capital, the post-office being only open one hour ere its departure. Stamps were obtainable, not at the office, but of a merchant a long distance off, who alone had the right of sale. The universal presence of the sewing-machine was the sole suggestion of progress. Nearly every house contained one. I observed, loitering around the custom-house wharf, some dirty, miserable-looking creatures, clad only in shirt and trousers and bearing rusty sword bayonets and cartridge boxes. These were soldiers of the regular army of Costa Rica! The entire force consists of nine hundred men.

Railway tracks lead through several of the streets of
Punta Arenas to huge coffee warehouses, which during
the season are full to repletion. The town is in exactly
the same latitude as Puerto Limon, and San José, the
capital, is but four or five miles south of a straight line
drawn through these seaports. A railway has been surveyed from port to port, but from neither end has the
work been pushed toward completion. From Punta
Arenas it extends but thirteen miles to a town named
Esparta. Only three trains weekly run between these
two places. The schedule time for leaving Punta Arenas
is 3 P. M., but it was 4 when we started. The pro-
jectors saw no necessity for building a station. A whis-
tle several times repeated gives notice that in twenty
minutes the locomotive will start. Our train consisted
of one passenger car and two freight cars. The engine
was made at Rodger's factory, Trenton, N. J.; the cars
were from Wilmington, Del. Only one engine being
employed on this section of the road, the risk of collision
was infinitely minimized. It would have been averse to
Costa Rican policy had not the ticket office been several
blocks from the point of departure. The fare was thrice,
and the speed one third as great as in the United States
for the same distance. The engine burned wood. Our
conductor was dressed in jacket and trousers of dark-
blue cloth, and a revolver bristled menacingly from his
right hip-pocket. We stopped but twice—once to get
water and once to make steam. At first the road led
through a tropically rich forest, peopled with birds of

brilliant plumage, but presently it turned inland, and whisked us from this leafy environment until we reached the terminus.

Esparta, half hidden by dense vegetation, lies seven hundred feet above sea-level. It was nearing the end of the rainy season, and the vegetation was at its rankest and at its deepest green. Upon one side of the ever-present plaza was a good hotel kept by an old Frenchman; upon another side stood the " church "—a miserable old shed enshrined in a pretty flower garden. From Esparta you may go by horse or mule to Alajuela, and thence by railway to San José, a distance of thirty-nine miles. We hired mules for our baggage and horses for ourselves and guide. The steeds of Costa Rica are very small, but tough and sure-footed. The road was wide, in part macadamized, in part badly paved. Coffee and the general produce of the country were carried chiefly in ox-carts. These are simply small oblong boxes, resting upon wooden block-wheels three feet in diameter. Each yoke of oxen pulls by means of a cross-bar lashed to the horns and forehead in such a manner that neither of the beasts can turn his head without the other, and even then only slightly. This cruel custom is practiced all over Central and South America. The drivers guide the oxen with iron-pointed poles, but the guiding is goading as well.

We left Esparta at daybreak. The road dipped into little valleys and out of them again, and leaped small streams upon firm stone bridges approached by long causeways. The country was but thinly settled and sparsely cultivated; in fact, but a twentieth part is thus redeemed. The bamboo houses were palmetto-thatched. Often at one end of a little veranda I saw a mud and stone oven, shaped like a bee-hive, and, like those in savage Africa, furnished with mortar and pestle for pounding corn. Sometimes that staple was piled high, but no vegetable patch was seen. The rainy season not being quite over, few travelers and little merchandise were in transit. We breakfasted at San Mateo, a hamlet a few hundred feet higher than Esparta. Here the rain fell in torrents during the rest of the day and most of the night, but, donning rubber leggings and *ponchos*, we crossed the Aguacate hills and reached the town of Atenas at 8 P. M. During the last hour we journeyed in total darkness. We passed the night in the public room of the hotel in company with eight other persons. Next morning we pushed on to Alajuela, reaching it by noon. The vegetation we passed was rich in mango, bamboo, papaya, bread-fruit, orange, guava, gourd (the calabash), palm (the royal variety), and tamarind. A handsome stone bridge took us across the Rio Grande, one of the larger rivers, whose upper waters were enriched by mines of copper, gold, and coal. A few miles north of Atenas are the gold mines of Aguacate. The chief cities of Costa Rica are situated on the highlands of the interior, and are comparatively near together. They begin with Alajuela, about three thousand feet, and continue with Heredia, San José, and Cartago, in a direction nearly due east. Cartago is about five thousand feet above the sea. Fifteen miles north of Alajuela is the twin volcano Poas, about nine thousand feet in altitude. Alajuela is a large town, laid out at right angles, with narrow macadamized streets and one-story houses. The country between it and Atenas is half forest and half pasture land. The classical names that abounded, such as Sparta, Athens, and Carthage, sounded strange to me, accustomed as I had lately been to towns and saints of Spanish nomenclature. In the center of the plaza of Alajuela was a handsome bronze fountain. On one side stood the cathedral, on another the cuartel, or barracks, and on a third the town hall. The railway from this town is a narrow gauge, with cars and locomotives of American make. At that date it extended only to Cartago, twenty-six miles off, whence a break of twenty-seven miles could be covered only by mule or horse. That distance traversed, the railway again appeared, and continued for seventy-one miles until it reached Puerto Limon, on the Caribbean Sea. All baggage is paid for extra in Costa Rica. From Alajuela to San José we passed through an almost continuous coffee field, this being the center of the best plantations. Our train accommodated many ladies in black gowns and shawls, though quite bonnetless, and men in jackets and trousers of dark cloth, wearing Panama hats. We alighted in an insignificant station where one-horse cabs were in waiting. I passed a square with a pretty fountain in its center, and caught sight of a marble monument, consist-

ing of a bust of the late President Fernandez, supported
on a pyramidal base. Clean macadamized streets ran between single-story houses with mud walls and tile roofs.
The shops that abounded resembled wooden boxes. The
two-story hotel that I reached was set off with the omnipresent bar-room and billiard-room, to say nothing of
the New York piano in the ladies' parlor.

The city of San José lies in the midst of a beautiful
valley. It is nearly level, with perhaps a gentle slope
toward the west. From the towers of the cathedral a fine
prospect may be had, more especially of the surrounding
hills, planted with coffee, sugar-cane, corn, beans, and po-
tatoes. It is a picturesque combination of tree and field,
cultivation and uncultivation contributing their diversi-
ties. Private properties are prettily divided by living
fences of cactus and wild pineapple. The city itself does
not offer much architectural variety. It consists mainly
of single-story houses, built uniformly, with low sloping
roofs, whence eaves project shelteringly over the sidewalks. A few churches, the President's house, and the
Government Palace alone break the monotony of the *ensemble*. The streets are right-angled, lit with electricity,
and macadamized or cobble-stoned. The sidewalks, from
one to four feet wide, are of brick, stone, or tile, edged
with curb and bordered with good gutters. The principal business street is named Calle del Comercio. Here
are the retail shops, which, when not small square boxes,
are long and very narrow. They contain large supplies,
among which sewing-machines and gay-colored garments

are prominent. The plaza is appropriately named Central Park, on account of its being near the middle of the city. It is a beautiful little inclosure, surrounded by a high and ornate iron fence and containing a fountain, fine beds of flowers, smooth-shaved lawns, neatly graveled walks, and a pavilion for the band. Orchids were interspersed among the trees, and splendid tame paroquets—yellow, blue, black, and gray—with clipped wings, were interspersed among both. To the east of the park was the cathedral, and to the south were the barracks. Hard by was Government House on Comercio Street. On the same street stands the market, a fine structure, occupying an entire square and well adapted to its purpose. Its quadrangular building is devoted to manufactures. Its open sheds and the intervening spaces of the interior abound with vegetable produce, and give elbow-room to the curious female butchers. Saturday is the grand market day. All classes barter or buy, and lay in enough to last until the following Saturday. The President's palace is a short block away from the Government House. It is a two-story stucco building, flanked by a solitary date-palm. In front a sentinel parades, one or two officers lounge, and a bugler and a drummer perform their duties. The drummer is a little barefoot boy with an apparently toy drum of apparently home manufacture. In fact the rank and file of the Costa Rican army are mostly boys dressed in blue-duck jackets and trousers, wearing caps, but neither shoes nor stockings, and armed with modern breech-loading rifles with sword-bayonets attached. The officers wear a blue-cloth uniform, and are so omnipresent as to seem to outnumber the privates. Guard-mounting and inspection in the morning and parades in the afternoon occur daily in the streets opposite the President's Palace. The military band always appears at these ceremonies, playing waltzes and opera-bouffe music. The city is policed almost wholly by boys, who wear blue uniforms and ungainly caps like those used in the Dutch army. Each of these adolescent policemen carries a small club of hard wood, and displays a silver button which indicates his official capacity. The police have but little to do in San José, however. It is an extremely well-ordered community, where crime and violence are almost unknown. The chief violence is that of the elements during the rainy season, which lasts about one hundred days. The rain begins every day at noon and continues with considerable energy until next morning.

On Sunday I attended military mass in the cathedral —a large structure with Doric façade and two towers and a dome above that part where the choir is located. The pediment over the main entrance accommodates a clock. Ascending a broad flight of steps, you enter between rows of Doric columns. The semi-cylindrical roof of the nave rests upon a double row of huge pillars. The side aisles are decorated only with paintings of " the stages of Christ." The light-colored tile floor is vari-patterned. All the interior gleams with white and gold. Inside the altar-railing are chairs of state for the President and the bishop. The altar itself is not particularly

grand. The military mass was the occasion of picturesqueness. The band was composed of forty instrumentalists, in blue coats and red trousers. To this con-
course were added a company of troops in blue, with
flashing bayonets, and a still more imposing array of officers in elaborate uniforms. The contingent of police-
youths was not without a sort of eccentric expressive-
ness. These detachments occupied the front and center
of the nave. The mahogany benches on both sides were
occupied by the "best" people—the men in dark clothes,
the women resplendent in many-hued skirts and mantles
of pink, lavender, yellow, and black, elaborately embroidered with flowers. None of the women wore hats, and
their dark hair, creamy complexions, and flashing eyes
were more dazzling than all else the cathedral contained.
No need of the golden neck-chains and ear-rings so afflu-
ently displayed. No use of the rouge which was *not* used
or of the powder that was. To invoke cosmetics for such
beauty would be like adding light to electricity or glory
to the Victoria regia. The poorer classes were also present—barefoot men in jackets, barefoot women in skirts
and chemises, with scarfs or mantillas. Light streamed
upon the assemblage through large upper windows, and
an occasional sun-burst brightened the stained-glass background of the choir. When the congregation knelt or
rose the effect was that of a thousand prisms. The band
played a selection from Lucia, the grand organ alternately threatened and cajoled, the priests intoned, the
people responded, and I stood spell-bound. The serv-

ice was brief, however. At its conclusion the military left to the tap of the drum, and marched gayly down the street to airs from La Fille de Madame Angot. On Sundays in San José the banks and the Government offices are closed, but most of the shops remain open.

In front of the cathedral, on both sides, are pretty gardens. Back of one of these stands the sacristy or small vestry, and back of the other the two-story dwelling of the bishop. The Government Palace is a plain two-story building on the Calle Comercio. It is built in a quadrangle, with a fountain in the center of the court. Down-stairs, facing the entrance, is Congress Hall, a small oblong room with a ceiling paneled in white and gold. Twenty mahogany desks are ranged in a semicircle around a chair of state for the presiding officer, surmounted by a crimson canopy. Beyond the desks are benches for the populace, and at each end of the room a small gallery is erected for ladies or for orchestras, or for both. Handsome crystal chandeliers depend from the ceiling. The walls are adorned with neatly framed portraits of Costa Rica's great men—presidents, generals, statesmen—among whom I noticed likenesses of Morazan, Carillo, Guardia, and General Bernardo Soto, the present head of the republic. The second story is occupied by the offices of the various secretaries. Two evenings in each week the military band plays in front of the President's palace. Stands, with candles, are placed for the musicians, and the people promenade up and down

The Breadfruit Tree.

the neighboring streets. This band succeeds best with dance music, native or foreign, such as is generally strummed on guitars with castanet accompaniment.

The "Savanna," which we one day visited, is a large level plain of beautiful and pathless meadow-land, which would make a splendid *campo de marte* for the army of a great power like Germany. Crossing its center at right angles are double rows of trees. The Savanna is the popular place for horseback exercise morning and evening. It belongs to the city, but is used as a general pasture-ground. From it may be seen the little towns of Alajuela and Heredia, their white walls shining brightly amid the dark-green foliage by which they are half enveloped. The Savanna is bordered by extensive plantations of coffee and sugar-cane, with a few farm-houses intersprinkled. Circling around are the enchanting hills which begirt San José, like a ring of verde-antique inclosing clustered opals. Away to the northwest arise the twin peaks of the volcano Poas; to the north looms Bomba; while to the east towers Irazu, eleven thousand five hundred feet high. The latter is now a dead volcano, but once it overwhelmed and destroyed the old capital of Cartago.

Since my departure there has been a series of destructive earthquake shocks in Costa Rica. Perhaps the worst of them was that which occurred on December 30, 1888. It is believed to have been caused by the eruption of the Poas volcano, which had been inactive for a number of years. An average of three slight shocks was felt

3

daily for several days after the first. Business during that time was almost entirely suspended, and the majority of the people in San José camped in the public squares, fearing that their houses would fall. Both the national Capitol and the beautiful and ancient cathedral fronting the little Central Park are in ruins, and many other buildings were injured, among them the presidential palace, City Hall, and National Post-Office. In San José eight persons were killed, and a much greater number injured. The damage reached the sum of two million dollars.

San José contains a number of hackney-coaches and some few private carriages, the former plying to and from the railway station, but most of the long-distance transit is made on horse or mule back, though very few women are thus seen, either on business or pleasure. At the large stables saddle-horses may be hired in any number, for any time, or may be permanently boarded. The horses of the country are, as I have said, small but very enduring and sure-footed. A very good one may be purchased for seventy-five dollars. Three newspapers are published—two dailies and a tri-weekly. None are printed on Monday. These publications are entitled La Republica, El Comercio, and La Gaceta. They are single sheets, about eighteen inches by twelve, and are sold, the two former at ten cents each and the latter at five. They contain editorials, telegrams, a local gazette, shipping intelligence of the ports of Punta Arenas and Limon, and a goodly variety of advertisements. La Gaceta is the official journal, published at the national printing-office, and containing the acts of Congress and the reports of the various secretaries of the Government, the municipal announcements, and so forth. Under the head of police instructions, the newspapers indicate such drug stores as take turn in remaining open all night. Journals that circulate between the various republics are not required to pay postage. Throughout Costa Rica a telegram costs only about one cent a word. English is much spoken in San José. One hundred Americans—that is to say, one hundred United States citizens—are found there. Next to these in number come the English, the German, and the French, in the order named. Many of the natives speak English, having been educated in the United States or England; not a few have added to their intelligence by extensive travel in Europe.

All the houses of San José contain pictures of saints. As a rule these are very gaudily colored, and inserted in cheap frames of wood or metal. They are always in active demand. When I first attended the market I saw a vender with a full assortment of them, in tin frames, and upon my returning, two hours after, I found he had sold the entire stock. A paper dollar of Costa Rica is worth but seventy-one cents, American money; and silver dollars (Peruvian and Chilian are used) are at a premium of five per cent. Vultures are here, as in all South American cities, the scavengers provided by nature. Early in the morning you see them sitting on the house-peaks, generally with wings outstretched to dry. During the day they leap about the streets in search of garbage and offal, fighting among themselves, and afterward sitting gorged and stupefied among the trees or upon the roofs. Their sight and scent are remarkably keen. Even before an animal is dead they may be seen coming from every direction, circling round and round, until they alight near their prey, where they are compelled to await the repletion of the miserable curs of the country, should a village be in the vicinity. These vultures, or zopilotes, as they are called in Spanish, are everywhere protected by the law from human assault.

Among the places of amusement to which we went was the Teatro Municipal, where we heard Suppé's three-act comic opera Doña Juanita given in fair style by a traveling company from Spain. This theatre, said to be the oldest in Central America, reveals from the street only a stuccoed wall rising to the height of a single story and pierced by several large doors. In the evening the ticket-seller sits at one of these selling tickets by candle-light—orchestra, $1.25; gallery, 40 cents. Crossing a little open court with a bar-room on the right, we had to stoop in order to thread the low passage leading to the orchestra. The place was usherless, but numbers painted in large size upon the backs of the benches rendered conspicuous the respective seats. The orchestra *fauteuils* were merely cushionless wooden benches placed inconveniently near together. Many of the audience carried cushions with them. The floor was paved with large coarse bricks, whose dampness invited countless fleas to luxurious revelry. The auditorium contained two rows of boxes and a gallery. The light both before and behind the curtain was furnished by kerosene. It is the custom for occupants of boxes to send or bring their own chairs. The band numbered twenty instruments, the leader playing with one hand and directing with the other. As usual in theatres of this caliber, especially those managed by members of the Latin race, the best understood member of the company was the prompter. He may be said to have given a good reading to every *rôle*. The effect was almost as if he were singing a duet with tenor, soprano, basso, or contralto, as the case might be. There was no solo where his voice was not heard, and he added a seventh to the sextet. We had gone late, well knowing that we were in one of those regions of delay where procrastination is not only the thief of time, without any one's knowing what becomes of the stolen goods, but also the soul of business. In the center of the second tier, over the entrance, was the President's box, draped with crimson cloth and faced with the arms of the republic. One of the proscenium boxes, intended for some of the Government ministers, was similarly distinguished. The uppermost proscenium boxes were not more than three feet square, and were located just beneath the ceiling, presenting a very eccentric appearance; but one person could be seen peeping from each of these, like a mouse peering from its hole. The Central American fashion with theatre patrons is to go half an hour or an hour late, and then to go with a rush. You frequently see people enter, deposit their wraps and coats on seats, and then return to the lobbies, the men to smoke, the women to chat. Men are rarely seen in the boxes. The latter are generally crowded with women and children. A man will leave his family in a box and take a seat with some male friends in the orchestra, where women are seldom seen. The men appear in coats of every cut and color except evening dress, the invariable accompaniment being the Panama hat. The women wear gay evening toilet and bonnets. The favorite colors for gowns are pink, white, blue, green, with low neck and short sleeves, flowers in the hair, *bouquets de corsage*, and a profusion of diamonds and other gems. Some of the younger were pretty, and would have been more so had cosmetics been wholly abjured. The upper classes of both sexes have very light complexions; the lower classes are darker. Meanwhile a cracked bell had twice signaled noisily from the stage. Nothing visible ensued. Finally, after a lapse of twenty minutes, the bell sounded again, the scattered audience rushed to their seats, and the opera began. The house was full. The Teatro Municipal being the only one in San José, and being open during only a small part of every year, audiences are always large and enthusiastic. A new and more desirable play-house was building, however. Opera is given only one night per week, that one being Sunday. Announcements are made by newspaper advertisements, a flag flying from the top of the theatre, and two rockets fired at 7 P. M. on the days of representation. The *entr'actes* are very long, but are hugely enjoyed, the audience instantly leaving the auditorium for the lobbies, the women to talk and walk, the men to drink and smoke, beer and cigarettes being in friendly rivalry. Outside the theatre swarm stalls and shops where cakes, sweetmeats, coffee, and liquors are sold for the refection of the humbler classes. The evening we were there the performance concluded at midnight, but sometimes it does not end for more than an hour after.

Very many of the Costa Ricans wear jackets without waistcoats, but with a bright sash around the waist. The stranger is startled at first by the vision of a barefooted man, otherwise neatly and well dressed. Another astonishing object is a woman in a skirt of dark color, but with the upper portion of her person attired only in a white sleeveless chemise. In the streets hatless women are seen with their hair down, though sometimes a man's Panama is worn, looking as if the woman had borrowed her husband's in a hurry—though no one is ever in a hurry here. Even the upper-class women go bareheaded in the streets. They dress gayly, wear high-heeled slippers or shoes, and occasionally carry sunshades. Even in very rainy weather they use no headgear, and little other shoulder covering than rebosas, or long, narrow scarfs. The singular separation of the sexes in the theatre has been already noticed. The same separation occurs everywhere, both in public and private. Very seldom do men walk with women in the streets. They are together, of course, in church, at parties, and at balls; but after a round dance the women huddle together in one corner and their recent partners do the same in another corner. In private parlors male visitors sit facing the ladies, never beside them; and even with the children of the same family, the boys are kept separate from the girls. Throughout all Central and South America you will find in every parlor a line of chairs extending in a right angle with each end of the sofa. One of these rows is for men, the other for women.

The Costa Ricans are very honest people. You do not need to lock your door in a hotel. Personal baggage is brought in cart from the seacoast to the capital without escort, or other attendant than the cart-driver, and almost always without loss or injury. Treasure is also sent to the coasts without escort. The people are very much more liberally disposed toward foreigners than are other Central American states, or than the South American states. Recently a Protestant American was allowed to be buried in the Roman Catholic cemetery of San José. The city contains a Protestant church, or chapel, where services are held every Sunday by a layman, the society of Protestant foreigners being, as yet, either unable or unwilling to support a clergyman.

One mile from the center of the city, on the west side, is the Panteon, or Campo Santo, of San José. A good broad sidewalk of stone slabs follows the road, bordered by coffee plantations, directly to the gate of the burying-ground. In front, on one side, is a large unkempt flower garden. On the other stands the grave of the late President Fernandez. In one corner is an octagonal vault, in the center of which lies the body of Jiménez, also a former President, with a recumbent figure of himself, carved in white marble. The cemetery is surrounded by high brick walls, and affords burial both in vaults and in mural tiers. The low cubical tombs reminded me strongly of those built by Mussulmans. Cypress and cedar trees abounded, but the grounds were in great disorder. The mural burials were against the inner face of the walls, and extended in four tiers, with the floral offerings and inscriptions common to all Roman Catholic countries. The open vaults contained small altars, with wreaths and conventional pictures of saints.

The International Club occupies a neat one-story building, and contains reception, reading, billiard, card, and bar rooms. Men can not remain men and be without billiards, cards, and drink. In the court was a tangle of beautiful flowers. The reading-room contained periodicals in Spanish, English, German, and French. The library, of perhaps two thousand volumes, was principally in English. German classics were found, however, in good force. In English, works of travel largely predominated, and I mentally praised the discrimination of the library committee in having provided a copy of The Land of the White Elephant. My *amour propre* was not a little flattered by finding it had been well thumbed. The new Palace of Justice is a neat one-story building, with the everlasting interior court, around which are grouped the offices devoted to the departments of Government. Mahogany and other fine woods are used in the furniture of these rooms. A few years ago an enormous Bull-ring of brick, at a cost of seventy-five thousand dollars (it is said), was built near the railway station. But bull-fighting not being to the taste of the Costa Ricans, the ring was abandoned, and is now devoted to the peaceful pursuit of picking and drying coffee. ×　slip 38

The national factory of liquors is not unworthy of a visit. The Government has the monopoly of the manufacture of *aguardiente*, vulgarly known as rum, made from the essence of the sugar-cane, compounded with various sweet *liqueurs*. *Guarapo* is the fermented juice of the sugar-cane; *aguardiente* is the distilled spirit. Of this latter preparation the natives are very fond—and foreigners are not invariably averse to it. On the hill near the railway station, on the eastern border of the city, is a high-walled inclosure which looks like a fortress. It covers about two acres, and contains the houses for the engine, the still, and the places where fermentation is carried on, as well as the residences of the superintendent and engineers, and accommodations for storage. You enter the grounds through a high stone gateway, whose pediment contains a clock. At the left are some offices, whence a custodian courteously issues to show you the premises. You are introduced to four large stills, manufactured in Glasgow on what is known as the "coffee principal." In this factory are employed an American engineer and two German and about twenty native assistants. Each of the fermentation houses holds four rows of large tanks, and each tank has the capacity of twelve thousand five hun-

dred bottles. The storage warehouses contain long rows
of tanks made of teak wood from India, and holding each
twenty-two thousand quarts. There were sixty of these
tanks, yielding a total capacity for one million three hundred and twenty thousand quarts. The present manufacture averages almost one million and a half annually.
Yet with this enormous production and consumption, you
rarely see any public drunkenness. These people, if constant drinkers, are also hard and regular workers. The
above is only a partial statement, however. Large quan-
tities of imported wines and beers are to be added. The
aguardiente contains twenty-two per cent of spirit, and is
sold wholesale at seventy-five cents per bottle. Of course,
it is milder than our whiskies, and very much more so
than our brandies. High on the hill back of the factory
of liquors are the city reservoirs. Water is brought in an
open aqueduct from a river eight miles distant. It is
thick, but, when filtered, becomes clear, and is regarded
as wholesome. The reservoirs are small, five in number,
built of cut stone, the walls being ten feet high and four
feet thick, and so curiously buttressed at intervals as to
have a mediæval look. The supply of water at the reser-
voir is greater than is needed—happy inhabitants of San
José—and the surplus is devoted to running the machinery of several factories. Mains convey the water from the
reservoirs to houses and fountains. There are also a few
hydrants for use in case of fire. The fire department,
however, is limited to one hand-engine. The water tax
is sixteen dollars per year.

The total distance across Costa Rica, from ocean to ocean, by railway and connecting cart-road, is one hundred and seventy-five miles. Of these, on the Pacific side, twenty-six miles are railway and thirty-eight are cart-road. On the Atlantic side, eighty-four are railway and twenty-seven are cart-road. The railway, however, is not completed. When it is the distance will be reduced to about one hundred and sixty miles. The railway on the Atlantic coast was expected to be finished in about two years. The track on the Pacific slope has been surveyed, but it is doubtful whether more work will be done there for some years. A complete railway across Costa Rica would be useful, but is not absolutely needed just at present.

I could not leave San José without taking a glance at Cartago, thirteen miles distant. Two trains run there and back daily. Passengers are notified by four sharp locomotive whistles twenty minutes before departure. The central division of the Costa Rican railroad runs from Alajuela to Cartago. At that point it is some day to communicate with the railway from Limon; and at a still more distant period it will be connected with Punta Arenas. Cartago is five thousand feet above the sea—one thousand higher than San José. The railway, consequently, has some very steep grades. It runs the whole distance along a mountain range which conceals deadly volcanoes and shelters beautiful valleys. The country is one vast coffee plantation, relieved with meadow-land and variegated with wood-crowned hills. It is not thickly settled. The dark and glossy leafed expanse of the coffee plantations is partially shaded by the long and undulating arms of the banana, and, nestled in the embrace of innumerable hills, presents a panorama of Arcadian peace. Near the line of the railway, a short distance from San José, is the country-seat of the President of Costa Rica. It is an ordinary single-story, quadrangular building. A small fountain plays at that side which opens toward the railway track. A few soldiers were lolling about the door. The President was not visible, but his beautiful wife was, and smilingly returned the salutation of one humble representative of a sister republic. The train was full of passengers, of both the first and the second class. The smoking of very inferior tobacco was universal, the women contributing to this end. I found Cartago to be a sleepy old place. It was formerly the capital. I stayed with an American who kept a good hotel on the principal square. In front stood the cut-stone foundation walls of the new cathedral. An enormous structure was indicated, and I did not wonder that it had never reached higher than six feet. Churches abound there, however, and none of them are of interest to a stranger. Cartago is cool, healthy, and uninteresting. It was soon to have a tramway, five miles long, built by the same American company that was to make one in San José, and entitled "The Costa Rica Market and Tramway Company."

The dawn succeeding my arrival in this place I went on horseback, two miles southeast, to the Aguas Calientes, or Hot Springs. They are in the valley below Cartago, just at the edge of a small river. A large brick hotel, with plenty of bathrooms, was in process of building. One large spring rises, boiling, directly from the rock. A huge cistern was built around it, and another one stood at a short distance above it, so as to have a necessary supply and pressure for the baths. The uncouth bath tubs were of brick and plaster. The water had a soft, agreeable taste, sulphur and iron predominating. It is much used, both internally and externally, and is said to be excellent for rheumatism and skin diseases. It resembles the celebrated Hot Springs of Arkansas. The hotel is to be named " Bella Vista," very appropriately, since it will command a magnificent view, including the volcano of Irazu, ten miles distant. Between Cartago and Aguas Calientes are the coffee estates of Señor Troyo, a rich planter. They constitute one of the finest plantations in Costa Rica. I made a thorough inspection of the entire place—beneficio, as it is called. In front of the two-story house stood curious statues, representing native Indians. Señor Troyo is an enthusiastic collector of Indian antiquities, and in his Cartago residence has a complete and rare collection. The plantation extends several miles along the valley, a road passing between the high walls of glossy green coffee-bushes, above which wave the banana fronds. Occasionally this road was lined with orange trees, among whose branches hung hundreds of those " globes in old gold." Nearly in the center of the plantation were the factories, the shelling and cleaning machines, and the patios, or great washing and drying ba-

A Costa Rican Owl.

sins. The machinery is turned by water. The buildings in general are provided with every necessary mechanical appliance of American manufacture. The basins, covered with cement, where the coffee is washed and dried, occupy several acres. Every part of the process may be inspected, from the place where the coffee is grown and picked to where it is packed in sacks and sent by rail and cart to the coast. The adjoining hills afford shooting — deer, ducks, and doves, being the few varieties. The neighboring scenery is remarkably fine, while the altitude of a mile mitigates the noontide heat and makes the night available for sleep. Irazu may be ascended to the rim of the crater on horse or mule. A descent into the crater is more arduous than dangerous. The trip up Irazu is frequently made in the dry season. From the summit, on a clear day, both oceans may be seen. The neighboring volcano, Turrialba, ten miles distant, as the crow flies, is much steeper, and has been seldom ascended. Irazu is dead, but Turrialba smokes a little.

On returning to San José I attended an exhibition drill of a local company of troops opposite the President's palace. The parade and manœuvres took place at eleven, Sunday morning, and were witnessed by the President and his ministers from the windows of his palace and by crowds of citizens in the streets. The exhibition consisted of the manual-of-arms (including bayonet practice without commands, and both with and without the music of the band), skirmish drill and blank-cartridge firing, and artillery drill with four little six-pound guns. There were thirty-eight men in the band, and thirty-five men, or rather boys, in the company! The former were seated in a row against the barrack wall, and played a great variety of waltzes. If I said they threw their souls into it, I should mean they knew the pieces by heart, and if I spoke of their playing from memory, I should mean that they executed more by faith than by sight. The soldiers were barefoot, the officers booted—and there were almost as many boots as bare feet. The evolutions were good with the exception of the marching, which was spoiled by the troops not keeping step. The variety of the evolutions smacked of many foreign countries, with a dash of native originality. The day was typically Spanish-American—mass in the early morning, then a military parade, next promenading and visiting in gala costume, finally, the theatre in the evening.

On the afternoon of October 19th we left San José for the seacoast and Punta Arenas, taking the train at five for Alajuela. There we spent the night, proceeding on our journey by horse and mule the following morning. Mules, owing to their greater scarcity, are more expensive to buy or hire in Costa Rica than horses. The average horse is very small, being hardly larger than a Saint Bernard dog. The mules, on the contrary, are generally large and stout, capable of carrying heavy burdens for long distances. The horses have a gentle and comfortable amble. They are almost always badly bowed in the hindlegs, owing to early overloading. The heads are very small, are accompanied with small ears, and look out of proportion to the body.

We breakfasted at Atenas, and stopped for the night at a private house about two hours' ride from San Mateo. The house was unfortunately destitute of edibles, but next morning we made a glorious feast with some milkless coffee, which was as welcome to us as Tanner's peach to him at the end of his forty days' fast. We reached Esparta about 2 P. M., the rain not being nearly so heavy as on the previous afternoon. The road, however, had been very steep and boggy, full of holes, and intersected with several small streams made dangerous by rapids. Passing the night at the Frenchman's excellent hotel, we reached Punta Arenas at nine the next morning, and waited for the steamer which was to take us to Corinto, Nicaragua, two hundred and sixty-two miles distant. This steamer makes but one stoppage—at San Juan del Sur, one hundred and fifty-six miles from Punta Arenas. When we went on board, on the 23d, she proved to be a small steamer of about fifteen hundred tons. A dozen nationalities were represented among her crew and stewards. The cooks were Chinese; the waiters Peruvians, Colombians, Guatemalans, Costa Ricans. Among the officers and crew were Americans, Englishmen, Mexicans, Scotch, Germans, Irish, etc. We left at midnight with a full list of passengers, who were bound for various ports in Central America, Mexico, and the upper Pacific coast. We were soon steaming off the northwestern coast of Costa Rica, the wooded hills of the province of Nicoya

4

and Guanacaste showing smooth outlines with occasional
rocky cliffs descending to the ocean's edge. No sign of
habitation was visible. To the northeast could be seen
the lofty peaks of Orosi, five thousand two hundred feet
high. After a while the hills became more bare, as if
composed of lava. Volcano cones came more clearly into
view, and the connecting ridges grew sharper and steeper.
Along the coast were many odd-shaped islands, some with
well-nigh perfect arches hewed through their cliffs by that
fantastic architect, the sea. One of these islands was exactly like a double-turreted monitor. Another counter-
feited a small brig under full sail. A third revealed the
crater of an extinct volcano peering hungrily above the
water. These were the last islands we saw as we bade
farewell to the Costa Rican shores, just previous to being
struck by a strong head-wind, which generally awaits the
traveler as he rounds the point of St. Elena. It probably
comes from the great lake of Nicaragua, which is twelve
miles distant by land from that point, and blows over the
split hills, whose occasional land-slides betoken volcanic
formation.

2. NICARAGUA.

San Juan del Sur is the southernmost port of Nicaragua on the Pacific. It is a small village near the edge
of a little semi-circular bay, which affords good anchorage
for a large steamer, but not for many at a time. The

hills are not two hundred feet high, and upon one of them, at the southern entrance, is a low lighthouse. About twenty miles to the north is the insignificant port of Brito, whence the proposed Nicaraguan ship-canal is to be cut to Rivas, on the great lake. From here northwest to Corinto the hills are monotonously even and low, and the nearest coast regions are almost a level plain. At daylight on the morning of the 25th we sighted the string of volcanoes named Los Marabios, or the Marvels, fourteen in number, extending from Lake Managua northwest to the Gulf of Fonseca, which, while it washes the limited southwestern shore of Honduras, separates the northwestern point of Nicaragua from the southeastern point of Salvador. Of the volcano range just mentioned, the famous and now smoking Momotombo forms the southern, and Viejo, back of Corinto, constitutes one of the highest and most notable summits of the northern end. A *fac simile* of "The Marvels" is stamped upon the Nicaraguan silver coins, and forms part of the national coat-of-arms. The sides and summits of these volcanoes are lava, and myriad streaks of brown and white, some higher, some lower, run into the forests that circle the bases and fringe the acclivities. Most of these eminences have sharp conic outlines, and vary in height from two thousand to six thousand five hundred feet above the sea. The foreground is low and level. About half-way between Corinto and Lake Managua it gives locality to the city of Leon, the largest in Nicaragua. A narrow-gauge railroad connects those two points. To the south the land was so low as to be invisible from the steamer. The long, broken line of the Marabios, blue and clear cut in the early morning light, was very beautiful. Some of the summits were lightly cloud-capped. The valleys, too, were filled with fleecy masses, like foam without a sea. The reader must bear in mind that while these repeated observations were being taken we had sailed away from San Juan del Sur, and were now entering the harbor of Corinto, which occupies a point on the coast in the north-west part of Nicaragua. From this position the sides of Viejo were seen, smooth, steep, and brown, and the crater distinctly outlined.

Corinto is a miserable little village, situated upon a low island just separated from the mainland. It has a small but good harbor, deep enough to accommodate a large steamer at anchor within a stone's throw of the shore. Cargo is taken to land in a great lighter, rowed by eight or ten men with huge paddles. In the center of the street which faces the harbor is a two-story building, surrounded with a veranda on both stories and used as a custom-house on the first floor, and as barracks on the second. On each side are buildings used by merchants, consuls, and consular agents. A little distance back is the railway station, whence two trains are dispatched daily to the interior. One at noon goes through to Lake Managua in four hours, where a boat may be taken very early in the morning for Managua, the present capital. It is connected by rail with Masaya and Granada, the only other large towns. At 3 p. m. each day a train goes as far as Leon, about half the distance to Lake Managua.

The people of Corinto are very dark, betraying strongly their Indian extraction. The principal hotel is a large, rambling, single-story shed—it deserves no better name—roughly divided into stalls. All Corinto swarms with mosquitoes. It is the chief port of Nicaragua, and at certain seasons of the year, as, for instance, when coffee is carried to market, it is much crowded. When I was there the harbor contained but one vessel, a small German bark. The locality is sandy, and cocoanut trees abound. Upon the broad, smooth beach the lighters are run, and the freight is transferred to the shoulders of half-naked men to be put in the warehouses. The miniature market contained little but an assortment of fruits and flowers. The latter are becomingly worn in the hair of all the women. Near the lighthouse, which stands on an island just off Corinto, is an ordinary wooden building extravagantly placed. It is built over a small excavation on the edge of a rocky cliff, and the excavation contains one old-fashioned gun mounted upon a "block" gun-carriage. From one of the windows of the house peeps the barrel of a smaller cannon. If these guns are intended only to fire salutes, their arrangement is singular, to say the least; but if they are meant for defense, no humorist could do them justice or injustice.

We left Corinto at noon for Momotombo, at the head of Managua Lake. The railway is narrow-gauge, and its equipment is North American. The engines come from

Baldwin's factory, Philadelphia, and the cars from Troy, New York. Upon the Nicaraguan as upon the Costa Rican railways, baggage must be paid for. One exception is on the railway from Managua to Granada, where twenty-five pounds are allowed free. This would not be much for a foreigner, but it should be remembered that in that climate the natives do not have many clothes or "personal effects." There are two classes of cars—the first-class having transverse seats, and the second-class parallel wooden benches. We had only a few passengers of the former class, but many of the latter. Among them the women were noticeable for their embroidered white chemises and gay-colored skirts, their jet-black hair braided and coiled upon the back of the head, and always prettily adorned with flowers. Dark, lustrous eyes illuminated smooth, olive complexions. The plumpness of these handsome women rendered them additionally pleasant to the view, while their constant chatting and laughter made them seem almost like happy children.

Once in the cars we crossed from Corinto to the main land on a long bridge, supported on iron posts, which conducted us southeast to Chinandega, a spread-out place, with long, straight streets, and houses mostly concealed by dense foliage. We stopped but little until we reached Leon, thirty-five miles from Corinto. The general character of the country through which we had passed was level, covered with a scrub-forest. It was thinly settled and sparsely cultivated, the principal products being bananas, corn, beans, and sugar-cane. The fences were generally "live," made out of wild pineapple. A peculiar kind of cactus was also thus employed, its round stems placed close together well suiting it for that purpose. Much of the land was carpeted with coarse grass, and a goodly number of cattle were browsing thereon. On the north side all the way to Lake Managua we had a clear view of Los Marabios, their streaks of gray sand and brown lava being well defined. In the forests were clouds of beautiful butterflies, but scarcely any birds. The station at Leon is a great shed. The town, like the others, is much veiled by verdure. From here to Momotombo, a distance of twenty-two miles, we ran through a much heavier and thicker forest, devoid of settlements. It took us four hours to go fifty-seven miles. There is some talk of continuing the railway from Momotombo, along the western shore of the lake to Managua, the capital, a distance of about forty miles. At present connection is only by steamer. Momotombo is an insignificant cluster of native huts, among which are conspicuous two small hotels, the railway station, and a long pier projecting into the lake. At the end of the pier are a little iron steamer for passengers, and a little wooden schooner for freight. Both go to Managua, four hours distant, down the lake. The town of Momotombo is notable for nothing save the picturesque beauty of its situation. To the east, and just across one of the heads of the lake, rises, to the height of fifty-two hundred feet, the symmetrical cone of the volcano Momotombo, always smoking and sometimes eruptive. The cone is more perfect than that of the celebrated Cotopaxi. It is smoother and sharper. The sides, one third the distance up, are densely covered with trees. Then come coarse grass, scoriæ, sand, and lava. These continue to the edge of the crater, whence the smoke sometimes ascends in an almost straight line, though it is often wind-blown into curves and spirals. The lake is dull-green, stirred by a strong south wind. As I sat upon the piazza of a neighboring hotel I could see the short, swiftly-succeeding waves beat on the fine sand of the black beach almost as fiercely as the storm-driven billows of the sea itself. The rapid roar and splash first delayed, then hastened sleep.

My first impression of Momotombo remains vivid. The afternoon was showery. Dark and heavy clouds alternated with a clear blue sky. In the foreground fretted the lake, yellowish-green in its general color, but crested with white-caps. Near by stood the forest, darkly verdant. Far to the right rose Momotombito, a small volcano, constituting an island by itself "with verdure clad" almost to its diminutive summit. Farther on in the same direction were the low hills of the western shore. To the north were the sandy volcanoes named Pilas and Asossoca. In rugged majesty, as though to gaze upon the spectacle of which it was itself a part, rose the mighty Momotombo, emitting smoke-wreaths from its naked crater, and casting the spell of weirdness over all that was lovely and romantic. Small time was allotted me for this unalloyed enjoyment. Clouds obscured the crown of Momotombo, a murky veil descended, and the character of the scene was changed.

It is said that Momotombo has never been ascended, owing to its steepness and the yielding nature of its soil. But the crater tips toward the east, and upon that side much lava has been thrown out, together with stones and scoriæ, so that there, at least, one could find a footing, though a precarious one. For at least half the distance progress would have to be arduously made through a path, which, if not already made by the lumbermen, would have to be cut by one's own machete, or hatchet. Of course, this could not be done in one day. The night would have to be passed upon the side of the volcano, and the work continued at sunrise. Once having completed the ascent, the descent could be effected the same day. About a year and a half ago lava ran down the eastern face of this volcano and fell thickly upon a neighboring town and into the lake. Hot stones were hurled high in air, the burning lava jets were particularly grand, and the reflection of the fire upon the clouds was Vesuvian in splendor. The eruption probably came from the bottom of one large central crater. The summit of the volcano is, in reality, perforated like a pepper-box lid, and emits steam and smoke from numerous orifices. Only about ten persons had the courage to remain in the neighborhood of this volcano during the outburst just described. Ashes like coarse sand fell in farm-houses twenty miles distant. Upon its sides, about a third of the distance up, are some sulphur springs, and near the

surface of the lake are fountains of the boiling variety.
At the foot of this volcano lives a man who keeps a
cattle ranch. The only other Nicaraguan volcano at
present active, or smoking to any extent, is Ometepe,
on an island of the same name—the largest island in
Lake Nicaragua.

The train from Corinto arrives at about 4.30 P. M., but
the boat for Managua does not leave until five the following morning. It was at that hour that we departed in
the little iron-screw steamer of fifty tons burden, the distance to be sailed being thirty-five miles. We passed
close to Momotombito. The color of the lake was a dirty
green. The navigation is everywhere good. Sometimes
the depth is as great as one hundred and fifty feet. Good
fish abound, particularly carp. Besides two steamers, a
schooner, and some lighters and canoes, no native craft
ply to and fro. The western shore is low, wooded, and
but little diversified. Upon the eastern shore extends a
long range of high, peaked mountains whose craters be-
tray their volcanic nature. These mountains are woody
below and grassy above. As we sailed away from Momotombo we had a clear view of a large round hole near the
summit of the volcano Pilas, which is variously said to be
bottomless and to be six hundred feet in depth. The
volcano is probably extinct. Near the center of the lake
is found the point of a long peninsula projecting from
its western side. Having rounded this, one or two of the
larger buildings of Managua appeared; but so depressed
is the situation of the town, so low are the houses, and so

dense is the foliage, that but little can be distinguished until one is very near. A large, oblong, curiously shaped hill rises in the background. It is covered with pasture, and conducts to a range of hills beyond, which, in turn, are in part cultivated, and in part occupied by forest and meadow. At the right I saw the white walls of what proved to be the two-storied School of Arts and Trades— the most capacious building in the city, as viewed from the lake. To the left were seen the crater-like summit of Masaya, the massive flanks of Mombacha, and the sharp cone of Ometepe in Lake Nicaragua. Along the beach were groups of semi-nude washerwomen, pounding clothes with their usual button-wrenching recklessness. At last we landed at a long pier, from which about every third plank had been removed. Several dilapidated hacks and lugubrious-looking horses were in waiting. As I passed through the town I observed that it was laid out with considerable regularity, though not at right angles. The houses were of mud. The streets were unpaved and of soft, sandy soil. There were no continuous sidewalks. The four drug stores I passed in quick succession indicated insalubrity. The grand plaza was anything but grand, with its uncut paths, its coarse grass two feet long, and its irregular rows of small mango trees. On one side stood the cathedral, by courtesy so called, with a façade of cut stone at once half completed and half dilapidated. On another side was the Government Palace. It covered an entire square, and contained the Halls of Congress, the President's resi-

dence, miscellaneous Government offices, and a library of
some three thousand volumes, mostly Spanish. A part
of the Government Palace was of stone—a sort of coarse,
volcanic rock, which may be easily taken from its bed
with an axe, but which hardens when exposed to the elements.

The Hotel Nacional, kept by an American, was near.
The court was full of trees and flowers. The breakfast
table was set in one of the lower corridors. The rooms
up-stairs were formed largely of Venetian blinds, and
contained hammocks, each of which seemed to hold a
lounger. Bird cages were suspended from the roof of the
corridor, and trailing vines shut out the sun and a little
of the air. Each bed-room contained from three to six
beds. Natives like this way of herding together. They
seem to have a superstitious dread of sleeping alone. Total
strangers—men with men and women with women—are
invariably companioned in this free and easy manner, and
robbery is almost never perpetrated. If you wish a room
to yourself in a hotel where other guests are staying, you
must pay extra. All the beds have heavy cloth mosquito
protectors, for mosquitoes are as intolerable in Nicaragua
as fleas are in Costa Rica. The bottoms of the beds are
generally canvas or crossed cords, upon which cool straw
mats are laid, and then one sheet and perhaps a very
light sort of blanket. At breakfast I made my first acquaintance with a very popular native drink—called *tiste*
in that part of the country. It is made out of maize,
ground and parched, and chocolate, mixed with sugar

and cold water, and served in thin calabashes of the size of ordinary tumblers. The calabashes are oblong, and preserve their balance by means of little wooden stands. They are often elaborately carved, and sometimes cost several dollars apiece. In a hotel it is the work of one woman to prepare the *tiste* for use at meals. The material is made into a long roll, like a sausage, the maize inside, and is thickly coated with chocolate. Pieces are broken into a gourd, sugar and water are added, the mixture is stirred into a thick foam, and is then served. The taste savors of both corn and chocolate, and is rather insipid, though thirst-quenching. The drink is not ferment, and answers as a refreshment merely. Natives use it in place of coffee. Sometimes you will be asked which you prefer—coffee or *tiste?*

In Managua I found it exceedingly hot during the day, but cool and comfortable at night. Showers are frequent, but brief and light. The streets are fairly well illuminated by kerosene lamps. In the center of the plaza was a wooden orchestra stand, octagonal in form and Moorish in style. On other sides of the plaza were barracks for infantry and artillery. A fine large building was being erected for the troops stationed in the capital. Near by was the picturesque little station of the railway that goes to Granada. The latter is larger and more important than Managua. So likewise is Leon. Granada and Leon have always been jealous of each other, each being anxious to become the capital. To evade the dilemma Managua was chosen. It has rapidly developed from a population of two thousand to one five times as large. The market-house occupies an entire square. It is a one-story building, as, indeed, are almost all the buildings of that place, on account of the frequency of severe earthquake shocks. At the corners the white walls are ornamented in plaster, above the entrances, with the republic's coat-of-arms. A vast variety of products is displayed, often incongruously grouped on the same stall. Things to eat and things to wear are in this queer juxta-position. Most of the sellers are women—many of them pretty, dressed in gay-colored skirts and white low-cut chemises, with roses and other bright flowers stuck in their raven braids. As before hinted, Managua has no fine public buildings. It is simply an extensive village. Foreigners are few. They are engaged in business, and are chiefly German and American. Only one newspaper is published—a sort of weekly official gazette. The silver dollars of Peru and Chili circulate at their full value here, as in all the other Central American states. There is no gold in circulation in Costa Rica, Nicaragua, or Honduras; and but little paper money in Nicaragua, and none in Honduras.

One day we rode out in a carriage to a little lake, named Tiscopa, half a mile west of the city. Several such lakes are in the vicinity, and all of them seem to occupy the craters of extinct volcanoes. Many of them contain fish good for eating. They are unconnected on the surface, and have no apparent inlet or outlet. Their water is dark-green and very deep. Lake Tiscopa lies a hundred feet below the surface of the surrounding country. It is circular in form. Its sides are steep hills covered with fine trees. In the early morning many of the men of the city go there for a refreshing swim. It is also the headquarters of numerous washerwomen, whose plump and dusky figures, bare to the waist, may be seen in every direction, near the shore. They usually stand nearly up to the middle in the water, facing the land, and pounding, soaping, rubbing, and rinsing the clothes on oblong blocks of lava-rock, in many of which are worn deep holes.

Managua is a rather dead sort of town. You never see so many people or such bustle in the streets as at San José. The railway thence to Granada is thirty miles in length. It is a narrow-gauge, with toy-like cars made in Central America, though the locomotives come from Baldwin's factory at Philadelphia. This road, like the one from Corinto to Momotombo, was not difficult to construct, there being no deep cuts or high fillings. In fact, the big lakes of Nicaragua are only about one hundred and thirty feet above sea-level. There are only four large towns in point of population—Leon, Granada, Managua, and Masaya. None of the cities of Central America are seaports, and the majority are located upon the higher and more healthy valleys and table-lands of the interior, from three thousand to five thousand feet above the ocean. Those I have mentioned are exceptions. The first three are about two hundred feet above sea-level; Masaya nearly four times that altitude. A small

river, the Tipitapa, flows from Lake Managua into Lake
Nicaragua, but owing to rapids is not navigable. By the
way, Lake Nicaragua is here called Lake Granada. The
town of that name is located at its northwestern extremity. Managua is at the southwestern end of Lake
Managua. The connecting railway passes through an
uninteresting country covered with scraggy forests, but
thinly cleared and peopled. Maize, sugar-cane, tobacco,
and beans are all that are cultivated. Half-way across
you see the large crater of the volcano Masaya, now extinct. Not far distant is a long, narrow lake, near which
stands Masaya, the only town of any importance on the
road. It being Sunday, the station there was full of
people in gala dress, laughing, gossiping, and promenading with true *dolce far niente* light-heartedness. The
black hair of the señoritas shone with cocoanut oil, and
their necks were hung with strings of pearl or chains of
dark-yellow gold. A large proportion (with the lower
classes, at least) was of French gilt. Sparkling stones
resembling diamonds palpitated in their ears, and rings
adorned nearly every finger. Their dresses were festooned
with lace and scarfs, white satin slippers shod their feet,
while an occasional cigar sensuously puffed smoke from
their ruby lips, and sent up fragile spirals of mist. At
the ends of the platform were vistas of palms, bananas,
and oranges, and the *ensemble* thus formed would be
worth being painted by many of our artists who go to
Algiers and Morocco in vain.

As we neared Granada station we perceived that it

was some distance from the town, which does not lie immediately upon the lake. Primitive hacks abound, and are cheap. The massive volcano of Mombacho stands a little lower down on the lake shore, to the right, and rises four thousand five hundred and eighty-eight feet. Still farther down the lake is seen distinctly the beautiful sharp cone of Ometepe, smoking, and about twice as active as it used to be. It stands on an island of the same name. Ometepe is a little over a mile high, and is still steeper and sharper than Momotombo. From Granada steamers run twice monthly down the lake and the San Juan River to Greytown on the Caribbean. At San Carlos, the beginning of the San Juan River, the lake steamer is exchanged for a smaller, the only one which can navigate the river's shallows and intricacies. From the station we drove along an unpaved street with disconnected sidewalks, their levels varying with various houses. The principal hotel, at which we halted, resembled a storage-warehouse rather than an inn. We were shown into a room forty feet by thirty, the ridge-pool of the roof being quite thirty feet above our heads. The floor was paved with square bricks. The doors were six feet by fifteen in size. The walls were three feet thick. No light could be admitted excepting by the doors, there being no windows. Six beds and two hammocks met the undelighted eye—and now we almost thought we were in a hospital. My companion was presently bitten by a scorpion, which we killed by way of retribution. The table where we took our meals was set in the inner cor-

5

ridor, one third of which was swept by the rain-storms.
Upon going to bed we resigned ourselves philosophically
to the combined attacks of fleas and mosquitoes. Mark
Tapleys only should travel in Central America.

Granada lies upon ground gently sloping toward the
lake. The rainfall is so heavy that, the unpaved streets
being very doughy, it is necessary to terrace them. The
terraces are connected by slopes paved smoothly with
enormous blocks of stone so as to be passable for carriages. The city is regularly laid out, though not at right
angles. The houses are built upon levels which are
higher than the roadways, so that the latter are always
two or three feet below the level of the sidewalks. These
are often neatly paved with white and black stone of local
manufacture. The city is lighted by kerosene lamps.
The stores and dwellings are much grander than those of
Managua. More wealth and culture abound. From the
top of the square tower of the old church of La Merced,
the first church in Granada at present, a fine view may
be obtained of the city, the lake, and the surrounding
country. There are no imposing public or private buildings. The view is simply that of a monotonous range of
red and brown tile peaked roofs, to which a very tropic
appearance is given by the appearance, here and there, in
courts and back yards, of cocoanut-palms, breadfruits,
mangoes, and bananas. The edge of the town is fringed
with grass-roof huts; then comes the intensely green forest. In the south rises Mombacho, wooded to very nearly
the summit. Upon the east lies the great lake, its diversi-

A Study of Ferns.

fied and indented shores clearly defined. To the south-east appears the beautiful cone of Ometepe. For more than a century this volcano was quiet, but during the last few years it has been turbulent—so much so on one occasion as nearly to destroy the town at its base. But human nature is the same in this respect as at the time of the flood, and when one is taken and the other left, the next generation seems to think it also may get left—though in a manner happier than that implied by the slang of the period. The low crater of Masaya is found to the northwest, but Momotombo is not visible. The grand plaza contains the begun cathedral and present barracks on one side, the market on another, and stores on the third. In the center is what may some time be a park. At present it contains uncut grass and a dry fountain. A few small trees have been set out. Opposite the hotel is an old stone gateway, dating from the time of the Spanish viceroys. Lions are carved on the façade, and its former owner's coat-of-arms over the gate. Other antiquities are the old Indian stone gods and earthenware implements and ornaments. Eaves project over the sidewalks, and protect from rain. Stores and dwellings are but one story, and the walls are of white stucco. The ledges of the enormous windows reach over the sidewalk like consoles, and are protected by semi-circular iron gratings sometimes elaborately carved. This arrangement allows the inmates to look out into the street in both directions—an opportunity enjoyed to the utmost by the gentler sex. The people generally are very inquisitive about the appearance and doings not only of foreigners but of each other also. Their talk is vapid and idle. True criticism is lost sight of beneath trivial gossip and personalities. They are not readers, and perhaps some allowance is to be made for them on account of their being shut in from much knowledge of the great world. In walking through the streets I observed that here the pigs disputed the offal with the vultures, those ubiquitous scavengers of Central and South American cities. If it were not for these animals, pestilence would result.

The commodious University of Granada is built in the usual quadrangular style, about an open court-yard. The "Museo" contains a small collection in natural history and archæology. The display of native antiquities did no justice to the interest of the subject and the resources at command. The small and not very interesting library was in fine red morocco bindings. The chemical laboratory was well furnished, but apparently not much used. The college has one hundred and twenty students—or had, at that time. They sleep in one long dormitory, the beds arranged hospital-wise. In all Nicaragua but one daily newspaper is published, and that is in Granada. It is called El Diario Nicaragüense. Its dimensions are thirty inches by twenty-four. It contains cablegrams and local news; but the latter not being marvelous, the lower third of the first two pages is occupied by a *feuilleton*, or *folletin*, as the Spanish say. The paper sells for ten cents per copy, or twelve dollars per year. The heads of advertisements are often very sensational, having nothing to do with the things advertised—a fashion which prevails, alas! elsewhere than in Nicaragua.

The vast difference in temperature at day and at night does not prevent abundant vegetation. At night a blanket is generally comfortable, though during the daytime the heat may be intense. The uneducated portion of the inhabitants do not understand the climate of places in the latitude of New York. Accustomed to rainfalls at regular intervals, they do not comprehend how we get along with our irregular rainfalls, which are liable to occur at almost any time. They wonder how it is possible to make the sun-dried bricks, of which they imagine our houses, as well as their own, are constructed. Apropos of this, an American, resident in Nicaragua for twenty-five years, told me an amusing story. Being questioned by a Nicaraguan on the subject, he replied that not only were our edifices of brick and stone, but that they were sometimes twelve stories high, and that Broadway was built up solidly on both sides for nearly ten miles. This more than satisfied the wondering interlocutor. The American congratulated himself on having successfully thrown light on a dark subject; but judge of his amazement when he overheard his questioner retailing the matter to some cronies, and stigmatizing him as "that old fool, Don —— "! Another native, not clearly understanding the difference between London and Paris, concluded, after serious rumination, that the former was like Leon, while the French capital resembled Granada!

On returning to Managua we took the little steamer

for Momotombo. We soon reached the peninsula where the extinct crater of Chiltepeque rears itself eight hundred feet high. The lake was alive with small fish. Occasionally an alligator sunned himself upon the surface. Tufts of vegetation abounded. Upon turning the peninsula we lost sight of Ometepe, but were compensated by the view of Momotombo and its little namesake, and the gray-yellow cone of Asossoca beyond it to the left. With Momotombo I was not less fascinated than at first. Its gigantic outline and magnificent evidence of its latent power were as weirdly suggestive as ever. I believe that, with endurance and pluck, its ascent is possible. We brought less stalwart qualities into play, however, by dining pleasurably at its base, and then took the train for Leon. Reaching there, we were obliged to trudge on foot from the cableless station to the hotel, a large quadrangle of buildings, with very high ceilings, thick walls, and doors like those of warehouses. The various corridors were used for dining-room, "sample-room," café, billiard-room, and *al fresco* sitting-rooms. Hempen hammocks of many lines were found in every room. Each sleeping chamber contained three or four beds. Among "extras" on the *tarifa* appeared the information, "He who wishes a room all to himself shall pay by special agreement." Manufactured ice was to be had in the café and at the bar. Perhaps this helped me to conclude that this was the best hotel in the republic.

Leon is not only the largest city in Nicaragua, but

also the ecclesiastical center, and the residence of the bishop. It has more churches than Granada, Masaya, and Managua combined. On the first morning after our arrival I was partially awakened by the crowing of the roosters—a universal and intense nuisance in this part of the world—and partially by a wonderful chorus of bells, compared to which the tintinnabulation celebrated by Poe was as nothing. Tinkling, tolling, booming, jingling, and jangling were fused into an infernal discord which murdered sleep as effectually as Macbeth ever did. I will not take an oath on the matter, but there appeared to be as many male chickens in Leon as Mark Twain estimated there were cats in Honolulu, and his calculation reached a million. The dogs, also, are a nuisance beyond description. They make night hideous with their howling, and after they have once awakened you, nothing can induce them to let you go to sleep again. However, bestowing anathemas right and left, I jumped up, and, dressing, started for the cathedral, but in anything but a devotional frame. It is a massive structure standing on the Grand Plaza, and filling an entire block. On the north side stood the two-storied municipal palace, a handsome building. The barracks were on the other side of the cross street. Instead of single sentries about a dozen soldiers there "mounted guard," to use the technical expression. What they were really doing was lolling on a bench, their muskets, only half supported, resting on the ground. The men were barefoot. A sort of coarse blue blouse constituted their attempt at uniform, but in fact the dress differed in each. In some of the rural towns the barracks are remarkable. In Momotombo a grass-thatched hutch answers that purpose; in another town a café-restaurant has been brought into requisition, retaining the old sign-board. Upon one side of the plaza stood the archiepiscopal palace, a two-story building, made of cut stone. Upon the remaining side were the post-office, the telegraph office, and some miscellaneous tumbledown buildings. The plaza itself was treeless and flowerless. The neighboring streets, in which were the chief stores, were unpaved and grass-grown. The interior of the cathedral — one of the largest in Central America—was very plain, but interesting on account of its curious old paintings and its carved choir, quaintly painted in oddly combined tints. The ceilings are semicircular and the walls are white stucco. From the towers you see the city massed together at your feet. Churches, large and small, alone break the dull uniformity. The country beyond looks superb. The plain whereon the city is built slopes gently from the chain of volcanoes on the east toward the ocean on the west. Around it stands a dense forest of beautiful tropic trees. From the center of the city the ocean and the volcano range are equidistant. Asossoca and Momotombo loom in the distance like the pyramids, through an atmosphere almost Egyptian in crystal brightness. All Leon rises but a story high, save only the cathedral, whose much-buttressed walls show the ravage of earthquake shocks. Thus caused was a great crack passing from tower to tower across the center aisle. In several smaller churches I observed similar cracks, which had originated in the same way. These smaller churches, unlike the cathedral, are cheap, tawdry, and primitive. In one holy water was exposed at three entrances in a china soup-basin, in the cover of the soup-basin, and in a wash-bowl!

In one of the shops I was shown that beautiful bird, the quetzal, which is to Guatemala what the American eagle is to the United States, though I am not aware that it ever screams quite as loudly. It is placed upon Guatemala's national escutcheon. It resembles the bird-of-paradise met with in the East Indies. The body is as large as a pigeon's, and three long, narrow feathers constitute the tail. The belly is crimson, the wings black, and the tail-feathers green and gold—the general effect of these radiant, delicate, and contrastive colors being almost iridescent.

The Central American people are apt to be very polite and attentive when it costs them nothing; on other occasions they are often selfish, annoying, and even rude. A man who will bow to you, or shake hands with you (if you will let him) half a dozen times a day, will talk aloud and laugh barbarously half the night even though he knows that you occupy a room separated from his by only a low partition. He will cheat you in a bargain after having expressed the greatest interest in your welfare, will help himself to the last bit of the choicest morsel while drinking your health, and while seeking to impress you with the habits of the good society in which he moves will eject upon the floor before you the water with which he has just rinsed his mouth — and so on *ad nauseam*.

On November 5th we went to Corinto and left next day by the Pacific Mail steamer for Amapala, sixty-three miles distant, the Pacific seaport of Honduras. At six in the morning the volcano of Chinandega was still in sight and we were nearing the mouth of the Gulf of Fonseca, the southern side of which is the Punta Conseguina in Nicaragua. The northern side is the Punta de Amapala in Salvador, while directly in front of us was the large gulf with its many islands. Beyond were the shores and the triple and quadruple ranges of Honduras. The headland to the right, upon entering the gulf, was a bluff coming down directly to the sea, with the barren and broken-headed volcano of Conseguina rising a little distance back to the height of about four thousand feet. Upon the opposite side was a similar volcano, called Conchagua, and far away in the interior of Salvador rose the great volcanic cone of San Miguel, shaped very much like Momotombo. At the foot of this volcano is the town of San Miguel.

3. HONDURAS.

The foreground of the coast of Honduras bore a more or less level aspect for some distance inland. At first it seemed merely a part of a great mangrove swamp. Then rose low hills covered with verdure, while beyond were seen separated cones and rough, precipitous ranges, barren, rocky, and yellow. Evidences of volcanic origin abounded. The mountains were diversified and worthy the study of an artist looking for new effects. We first passed some barren rocks named Farallones, their sides worn into vast arches. Then we coasted along large, green, conical islands, sprinkled with a few straw-thatched huts in half-cleared spots near the sea. The numerously indented Gulf of Fonseca accommodates half a dozen of these conical islands. The view of Chinandega from the north was fully as impressive as from the opposite direction. Many small rivers and one large river—the Rio Choluteca—feed this expansive gulf. Upon the Choluteca (called the Rio Grande upon its head waters) stands the Honduran capital, Tegucigalpa. The river is long and winding, but navigable only a short distance from its mouth. The cone of Tigre Island rose before us. Upon its northern side, protected from the great ocean swell, stands the little town of Amapala. Tigre Island is so called from the number of tigers which were once found there. This animal is now found upon the neighboring and much more barren island of Sacate Grande. To the west, in the rear of a number of islands, stands the town of La Union, in Salvador. Directly ahead, on the main land, and near the outlet of the Nacaome River is La Brea. Around a point to the eastward is found the sole remaining settlement upon the Pacific seaboard of Honduras, namely, San Lorenzo. La Brea is on the main road to the capital, and to this road another one from San Lorenzo leads. Through these two places all the imports from the Pacific side must enter the country. At Amapala is the custom-house. Passengers may be transported hence, in large sail-boats and canoes, to La Brea in about four hours, and in five to San Lorenzo.

In the roadstead of Amapala were anchored a small German bark and one of the little steamers of the Spanish Marquez del Campo line, recently started. The town, which is very small, is crowded in between steep hills, and is prefaced with a pretty beach of yellow sand. The green gulf, the yellow beach, the white town-walls, and the lush mountain foliage make a beautiful picture. To the right, shaded by cocoanut-palms, stands a white marble statue, erected in honor of the famous Honduran patriot, Francisco Morazan. It is surrounded by a low iron fence, the posts of which are topped with figures representing green parrots with red breasts and long tails. The invariable barracks next invite the view. At the end of a long wharf stands the *aduana*, or custom-house. The front street is shaded by mango and other trees, under which, and in the adjoining corridors, near the custom-house, the market is held. A few streets back and higher up, in a sort of plaza, is a very quaint church, with three towers on a line with the façade. These towers are pierced with small green windows, the edifice itself being of the whitest white. When I mention the large, uncompleted and unused barracks on the extreme left, I have indicated all the prominent architectural features of Amapala. A few Germans are engaged in business there, and several other foreign nationalities are represented by consuls and commercial agents. Passengers are taken ashore in dug-out canoes and sail-boats covered with curious awnings, and cargo is rowed in large lighters by six or eight men, using rude paddles fastened to long poles. The men handle these standing, and throw their whole weight upon them. The wharf not being in good repair is not used. Boats are run as near the shelving beach as possible, and both passengers and freight are carried on shore on the boatmen's shoulders. For ladies chairs are provided, which are carried between two men. We landed in the midst of an animated scene. A small band from the barracks was on the sea-front, playing a lively quickstep—not, as I was pleased to observe, the everlasting Boulanger March. A captive monkey was swinging from a neighboring veranda. Gayly attired market women were chattering and chaffering as only those people can. A few foreigners, dressed in coolest white, were rushing about in business haste— "hustling," I might almost say—just as foreigners do in those hot climates until experience has persuaded them that it is best to do things slowly. The view from the

front street of Amapala is very pretty. Before you is the
yellow-grassed and irregularly shaped Sacate Grande isl-
and, and to the left islets aglow with emerald are scattered in every direction. On the mainland odd and
broken ridges and peaks rise in terraces. As soon as you
reach the beach, you notice small houses standing upon
posts, which are closely connected by stout palings.
These are not boat houses or lookouts, but bathing
houses, and sometimes their roofs are frequented in the
cool of the evening, whenever there happens to be such
an article about. The water hereabouts is infested with
sharks. Hence the necessity of the bath-houses.

We had no difficulty with the custom-house inspectors,
and made arrangements at once to be taken to the mainland, so that we could start immediately by mule for Tegucigalpa, about ninety miles away. Travel was by cart-
road, described as good, but very dusty in the dry season.
Just then, at the end of the rainy season, it was tolerable,
though, of course, somewhat boggy. We wished to telegraph ahead for our mules, but on going to the telegraph
office, a Government institution, we learned that business
for the general public was not transacted until noon.
Returning at that hour we were told that the official had
not yet come back from breakfast, and our telegram was
not finally dispatched until 1 P. M. The office closes at
three, so that business hours are exceedingly abbreviated
at Amapala. It was thought by a resident merchant that
we would not be able to get mules at La Brea, the most
frequented point of departure, a small village where there

is one hotel, so called. We therefore telegraphed to Pespire, a point inland, on the road, to have mules sent to San Lorenzo. This was a little further from us, by boat, but nearer than La Brea by road. The wind promised to be favorable, but it would be necessary to have the assistance of the tide also. As a rule, no mules are kept at La Brea, since passenger travel to the interior is very small. Natives and foreigners living in Honduras usually own animals, and therefore are not incommoded and delayed like strangers.

The canoe we hired was hollowed out of a single great trunk. The flat bottom and the steep sides rendered it pretty stiff. It was more than twenty feet long, and was four feet wide. It carried a small sprit-sail, but owing to the irregularity of the breeze the men, three sailors and a captain, relied greatly upon their oars. Our seats were across the bottom of the boat, using the side as a rest for our backs. Rowing along the shore of Tigre Island, which is now a mass of lava rocks, now a pretty beach of smooth sand, we soon got beyond land, and a good breeze then wafted us briskly to the northward and to San Lorenzo. We passed splendid views of mountain ridges, volcanoes, and islands. As we neared the mainland we saw that it was covered with tall, thin mangrove forests. At last we got into a long narrow bay of smooth, dark water. The dipping oars stirred up phosphorescent masses, which glittered like finest silver. The sun went down in a fiery blaze, and afterward the twilight was shot and fluted with the most gorgeous tints and shades, reflected over mountain, cloud, and sea. It was quite dark when we reached San Lorenzo, and drew our boat up on the beach. The place consisted merely of two wicker-sided, tile-roofed warehouses, belonging to one of the silver mining companies of the interior, near Tegucigalpa, and partly filled with working material. A few small and wretched huts were in the neighborhood—and this was San Lorenzo! It was flat and swampy, and full of mosquitoes, gnats, and fleas. The miserable inhabitants were suffering from fever. We found neither food nor accommodation. Hiring a couple of hammocks from one of the huts, and hanging them in one of the warehouses, we tried, with but small success, to get a little sleep during the very hot night. Some of the people were engaged in salt manufacture, there being a large heap of very coarse, crude salt in one of the sheds. More wretched-looking creatures I have rarely seen. A dozen of both sexes, and several generations, live in one small room, the sides of which are made of twisted sticks. They possess almost no domestic utensils. Their fireplaces are simply oblong holes in the top of a pile of stone and mud, with a smaller connecting hole, used as a draught, below. A pot, a tin pan, an earthen jug, and a gourd, complete the kitchen outfit. Their food consists of corn made into tortillas, or thin, half-baked cakes. Their few clothes are filthy. They are very ignorant, very lazy, but quite hospitable— that is for a " *gratificacion*." They are good-natured and lively, and this, in fact, seems to be the case with the lower classes of mestizoes all over Central and South America.

Our telegram was forwarded to a man at Pespire, whose business it was to expedite travelers and luggage upon the road. Pespire is twenty miles from San Lorenzo. The dispatch having been sent at 1 P. M., as previously stated, we had expected to find our mules awaiting us, or, at least, had expected they would arrive ere midnight. Imagine our surprise at being told that we need not expect them before to-morrow noon, or, more probably, three or four in the afternoon! Thus it is with everything in *mañana* (to-morrow) land. Time is the solitary article with which the people seem well supplied.

They call it ninety miles from La Brea to Tegucigalpa, and a little less from San Lorenzo. The general direction is northeast. As soon as our mules arrived, at 3 P. M., we started for Pespire. The animals were small and tough. Mine was about as large as a St. Bernard. A good one is purchasable for twenty-five dollars; a good horse for ten dollars. Our mozo, or servant, went ahead on mule-back. Our arriero, or muleteer, went on foot driving our pack-mule. This man was dressed in cotton shirt and drawers, with an enormous straw hat. A huge machete was strapped to his waist. An iron cup completed his outfit. Calabash trees abounded amid the scrubby timber of the poor pasture-land. We passed many fine oxen and cows, most of them for home consumption. We met few travelers but many mule trains bound for the coast, to take goods thence to the mines. A good road, I should have said, extends from San Lorenzo to the capital. It is traversed by carts in the dry

6

season; by mules at other times. The latter mode requires two and a half or three days. For freight by cart a week is required. The country is so rough and hilly that a railway could be built only at great expense, if at all. Hours ere we expected to reach Pespire the rain fell in torrents; it grew quite dark, and we sought shelter for the night in the first hut—a miserable building, twenty feet square, surrounded by a fence in which were corralled cattle. The sides of the hut were made of the slender limbs of trees, sometimes two inches apart. Rain and mosquitoes came in. There was no window, and the door was narrow. The owner was rich only in cattle and in his fields of maize and plantain. The floor was of earth. A fire burned in one corner among some stones, which sustained a kettle and a tin pot. A few cups and earthen bowls completed the utensils. There was no chimney, but the smoke found egress through very open sides. Three bedsteads were each covered with a network of hide, and this again with an ox-skin and a blanket. A hammock was also present. Tables and chairs were absent. Meals were eaten from a shelf. Fifty odoriferous cheeses adorned the rafters above. Maize in the husk was heaped up. Articles for manufacturing cheese completed the equipment. Chickens, pigs, and dogs entered *ad libitum*. Here we passed the night in company with the man, his wife, two grown-up daughters, two small boys, and a baby. The family behaved kindly to us, and we distributed ourselves as circumspectly as we could in such narrow quarters. Ten human beings, four dogs, twelve chickens, three pigs, and innumerable insects wore the weary night away. We went to bed supperless. At breakfast we had corn-cakes, cheese, and bad coffee—and were glad to get that. We left at daybreak, and reached Pespire at 9 A. M.

Pespire is a small village grouped about a plaza which has the regulation church, with white dome. We breakfasted at a private house, there being no hotel. Our next objective point was Sabara Grande, much of the road toward which was lined with flowers of the morning-glory and honeysuckle type. The passing natives greeted us with "*Adios*," meaning both "How do you do?" and "Good-bye," as well as "A pleasant journey to you." The woods abounded with gay-colored birds, the road and river banks with brilliant butterflies. The wretched village, San Antonio de Flores, was on our left, and the river Moramulco showed its bed to be full of rocks and slippery stones. A scow, we noticed, is used for travelers and merchandise in rainy seasons. A stout rope is stretched from bank to bank, and the boat is moved by another rope attached to this one. A few huts on each side constitute the village of Moramulco. As far as La Venta we followed the valley of the Nacaome River. We crossed this river several times, and found it from fifty to three hundred feet wide. Its current is broken and swift. Its shores are of lava-rock and large and small pebbles. At La Venta, a little village on a steep hill-side at the extremity of one of the great valleys, we rested for the night in a private house, no public one existing.

Daylight of November 9th found us "over the hills and far away," getting splendid views of valley and volcano. Chinandega and San Miguel vied with each other, and the great bay of Fonseca remained sentineled by Conseguina and Conchagua. We now entered a thin forest of pitch and yellow pine. The air grew rich with balsam. The scene put on the aspect of the temperate zone. The road was not too steep and was hard and smooth. We breakfasted at Sabara Grande. This place lies near the bottom of a valley. It is the largest town on the highway from coast to capital. Upon the plaza is an old church with good façade. The place lacks a hotel, but meals may be obtained at a private house. A single telegraph wire accompanies the road from La Brea to Tegucigalpa, and there are three telegraph stations. The latter serve at the same time as post-offices. The mail is carried on foot, one man making the entire distance between the two places in forty-eight hours. The mule-road allows of many short cuts. Leaving Sabara Grande, we began the ascent of the Lepaterique Mountains. After passing these we crossed the still higher range of Ube, which brought us to the plateau whereon is the province of Tegucigalpa. The pine forests now gave place to meadows of fine grass, upon which numerous sleek cattle browsed. Many trees were a mass of orchids. Occasionally the ground was rocky, and covered with odd-looking varieties of cacti. It became cooler, for we were now four thousand feet above the sea. We found a good deal of marshy and level pasture-land, and rode through large groves of oak, whose limbs were hung with Spanish moss. This recalled the celebrated grove of Chapultepec near the city of Mexico. Occasionally we saw farmers using a plow as primitive as that of the ancient Egyptians—consisting of a wooden prong which did not seem to tickle the ground sufficiently to make it "laugh with harvests," as Douglas Jerrold saith. Stone walls replaced tree and cacti fences. The inhabitants, however, were poor specimens of humanity. Leaving the range of Ube, we proceeded down hill upon the best road I had ever encountered in Central America. It would have done no discredit to New York's proudest park. Nearly all the streams were spanned by massive stone bridges. A roofed wooden bridge crossed the Rio Grande and another the Guaserique River. As we neared the capital, of which we had obtained an appetizing glimpse, the short twilight faded into a dark rainy night. The white color of the smooth road enabled us to pursue our course, accompanied as it was by myriads of fireflies. These benevolent pyrotechnics of nature lighted us on our way. At last, at eight in the evening, after having been in the saddle for nearly thirteen consecutive hours, we reached that part of Tegucigalpa which lies on the west bank of the Rio Grande. After some perambulation, we crossed a large, paved, arched bridge, which took us directly into the heart of the city and to the Hotel Americano, where we obtained very welcome shelter for both man and beast.

After about fifteen minutes' walk north from the great plaza, in the center of Tegucigalpa, you arrive at the leveled summit of a little hill, which runs precipitously in the direction you have been taking. It is named La Leona, and from it the best view may be obtained of Tegucigalpa and the neighboring country. A large space has been graded, and the face of the hill will eventually be protected by a massive stone wall. In the center of the summit stands a large, octagonal, wooden pavilion, well provided with benches. A number of seats ran along the brow of the hill. Flower-beds and paths were being constructed. The road zigzags up in a grade sufficiently easy for a carriage, though horseback is the favorite method of ascent. A heavy stone wall protects the dangerous side of the road, and is a prominent sight from the city. The view obtained from the back of the Lioness is remarkably engaging. The country is hilly and is equally divided between wood and pasture land. Two distinctly marked valleys, however, present level bottoms and accommodate, at their intersection, the city of Tegucigalpa, built upon both sides of the Rio Grande and upon one side of the Rio Chiquito. The fine arched stone and brick bridge which we crossed in entering the city spans the Rio Grande and connects the two sections of the city. This river hardly bears out its grandiose title—at least, according to the ideas of one fresh from the land of the Mississippis, Missouris, and Ohios. At this point it is a boiling brook of foam, one to two hundred feet in width, its bed full of rocks, smooth stones, and gravel. The Rio Chiquito is merely a brooklet. In the rainy season both streams grow comparatively large. The Rio Grande runs

Statue to Morazan in Tegucigalpa.

north and south just here, and that part of the city on the east bank is Tegucigalpa proper. The suburb, called Concepcion, consisting mostly of two long streets, stands on the west bank. Ox-cart roads run from here to Comayagua, the second largest town, and to some gold and silver mines. The other roads are merely mule trails. Tegucigalpa may be said to be at the bottom of an amphitheatre of hills. It is one of those miniature cities in which civilization and primitiveness are curiously blended. The houses are mostly of mud and one story in height, though in the vicinity of the central plaza some of them have two stories. The manner in which the town is laid out is not irregular. The streets are narrow and roughly paved with cobblestones, sloping toward the center, thus providing that merely surface drainage which is so unsanitary. The sidewalks, though narrow, are paved with blocks of stone or brick, and the city is lighted with kerosene lamps. It is policed by boys and young men, who wear suits of blue cotton duck and large straw hats, on which is a band marked, in large letters, "Police." These policemen are barefoot. Their jackets bear their respective numbers.

Tegucigalpa has three pretty little parks, containing flowers, trees, and paths, together with busts and statues of distinguished Hondurans. The plaza—always "grand plaza"—is named Central Park, like that at San José, Costa Rica, and includes a very good bronze equestrian statue of Francisco Morazan, erected by the country. The marble pedestal is lofty. On one side a tablet bears an appropriate inscription. Another side reveals a bronze tablet, picturing spiritedly, in high relief, the Battle of La Trinidad, fought in September, 1821, and in which Morazan bore so noble a part. On the east side of Central Park is the massive cathedral, occupying an entire square. The imposing façade is surmounted by two towers, in one of which a clock marks the time, of which, as I have already explained, Hondurans have a supply more than equal to the demand. The front is relieved by niches, enshrining carved figures of saints. The cathedral has a long cylindrical roof, with a graceful dome over the altar. Confession boxes, side altars, and old paintings abound inside. The principal altar is of carved wood, covered with rich gilding, with the central "Holy of Holies" in fretted and tinseled silver. There are three or four smaller churches, but none of them are of special interest. The dwellings were better than those of the other cities I had seen. The exteriors were plain but the interiors were well furnished and lavishly ornamented. The general features resembled those I have already specified more than once, and henceforth if I do not mention them again, with respect to Honduras, Salvador, and Guatemala, it will be because no great difference exists between them and those found in Nicaragua and Costa Rica. In Tegucigalpa the houses, though of only one story, are very high and the doors very large. The windows extend to the sidewalk, and have iron gratings outside and wooden shutters inside. The city is the capital and the mercantile and ecclesiasti-

cal center. Many of the keepers of the smallest stores—
and all are small—speak English. (The goods are the *ne
plus ultra* of heterogeneity.) American sewing-machines
are found in mud huts as well as the houses of the rich.
In cabins devoid of crockery and furniture this invention
is present ! The contrasts here are many and very great.
Half-naked men peddle water in casks beneath handsome
bronze statues erected to patriots. Poor women use coins
for weight, and wooden and string scales in the neighborhood of stores which display expensive knickknacks,
Parisian millinery, and elegant jewels. The predomi-
nance of the mestizo element, however, makes the place
merely a big Indian village. But there is a university
and many schools. No paper money circulates here or
in the rest of Honduras.) Tobacco and aguardiente are
Government monopolies, generally farmed out to two
men. The aguardiente is retailed at seventy-five cents
per quart. Cigars are sold by Government by wholesale
at half a cent each.

On the evening of the day following our arrival, we
went to the Teatro Nacional, temporarily located in the
university. The latter and the presidential palace occupied two sides of a little park which contained marble
busts of Cabanas and Reyes, respectively a soldier and a
priest, both famous in Honduran history. (The theatre
occupies the large inner court-yard of the university.
The floor is of earth, the ceiling of canvas. From the
latter depends a glass chandelier, which accommodates
precisely four tallow candles. The rest of the theatre is

lighted by kerosene. Above the level of the orchestra is a row of boxes. In the center of the gallery, covered with a crimson canopy, is the box reserved for the President. The flags of Honduras ornament the sides of the stage, above. A military band of thirty pieces, under an American leader, furnished the music. This band consisted of young boys, barefoot, with ill-cut, unbrushed hair, and no attempt at the wearing of uniforms.) The audience was small, Sunday being the gala night. The general appearance was precisely like that I have previously indicated. A Spanish company performed comediettas, with long intermissions. About a dozen Americans were present, some living there, some from the neighboring mines.

(The police force of Tegucigalpa consists of twenty-four boys or young men. They are under charge of an American, who told me (they learn and perform their duties readily—the more so, perhaps, as unlike too many of our New York policemen, it is not necessary for them to acquire the art of insulting, assaulting, and maiming inoffensive or but venially offensive citizens. They are paid one dollar each per day. The delinquencies committed are chiefly petty thefts. There was but one murder in a whole year, and this resulted from a drunken brawl. Capital punishment does not exist. Death by electrosion—a word which has been recently suggested to express execution by electricity—has not been introduced, and ten years' imprisonment is the severest sentence of the law. It is difficult to convict any one of theft.

try and in the application of capital were due to his talent
and energy. Politically, he is an advanced Liberal, and
is said to have an imperious will. He needs it, for there
is a strong Conservative element in Honduras. For instance, a citizen dropped in while we were speaking of
the mineral wealth of the country and the foreigners engaged in mining. The new arrival thought that foreigners should not be encouraged, inasmuch as they were
taking all the precious metals out of the country. " Well,"
answered President Bogran, " as an example of what the
foreigners have done, let me say that when I obtained
power a few years ago the mail-carrier could bring, in
addition to the mail, all the silver down to the coast; but
now the American company of one mine alone have employed in their work two thousand mules. We, at least,
can not and have not used our mines, and it is better
that we should have the money and business that foreigners bring to the country. Honduras," he continued,
" is very rich, not only in minerals, but in agricultural
products, for it has vast plains but little above the level
of the sea, and hills four or five thousand feet in eleva-
tion, thus yielding a wide variety of produce. But Honduras requires interior communication. It needs some
railroads, but it also needs more cart and stage roads.
It is a very hilly and generally uneven country. A large
portion of the population dwell far inland. The mule-
teers are sworn opponents of railways and stage lines."
The President, however, is determined. He says he will
make a beginning of putting the road in good order from

La Brea to Tegucigalpa, and starting—and subsidizing, if necessary—a line of diligences upon it during the coming year (1888). Reference was made to the enormous debt incurred by Honduras in starting, without building more than thirty-five miles of a great interoceanic railway from Puerto Cortez, a splendid harbor on the Atlantic, to Amapala, or rather La Brea, on the Pacific. He said it was entirely an English concern, that Honduras never had the handling of one cent of the funds, but, believing that everything was regular, had merely guaranteed the money. Affairs were very badly managed, however, and it is a matter of history how all came to grief, and Honduras became saddled with a debt of thirty-one million dollars, on which she has never been able to pay any interest, but which the President is endeavoring to consolidate and otherwise adjust. He added that when these and some other matters were arranged, a Chicago company was willing to build the railway. He said that the poverty of Honduras was to be found in the ignorance of the masses of the population, which prevented them from making the most of their environment. He therefore favored immigration, and was especially partial to Americans. We found General Bogran's entire conversation patriotic and sensible. His record shows in part what he has wished to do, and well would it be for Honduras were more of his ideas adopted and carried out. He is in advance of his times. While this interview was in progress, three barefoot boys of the lowest class walked in the room, threw their hats on the floor, and reverently bowed to the President, who rose at once, cordially shook hands with them, and asked them to be seated. It was a fine display of democracy—a notable example of the free-and-equal dogma worked out to ultimate conclusions in a Central American republic.

On November 11th we left Tegucigalpa, but not before having heard the Boulanger March played from a private house. We reached Sabara Grande in the middle of the afternoon, and spent the night there, leaving at daylight next morning *en route* for Amapala, arriving at Pespire at 3 P. M. On the way I observed that in some of the fields the men were thrashing out the rice, taking a handful of straw at a time, and beating it upon a small platform surrounded by a fender of plantain leaves. Near most of the haciendas, or farm-houses, were great square hen coops, raised eight or ten feet from the ground on posts. This was to protect chickens from prowling foxes. On the banks of the Nacaome River, a short distance south of Pespire, were masses of black basalt, tilted on end, and standing in terraces, like those in the Giant's Causeway, Ireland. In coming down from Tegucigalpa we had met much freight going into the interior. This was mostly for the mines—and for those of Rosario and San Juancito, more particularly, to the east of the capital. Trains of eight or ten mules had a mounted mozo ahead, with two or three boys as drivers. The mules were noticeable as large, fine, fat specimens of their kind. During our journey heavy showers, accompanied by thunder and lightning, fell every day about 2 or 3 P. M. Small

General Bogran, President of Honduras.

se
too

rivers and lakes were thus improvised. The enormously large rain-drops fall on mule, rider, or pedestrian almost like the sting of a whip, but the showers do not extend over much surface or last for a long time.

We left Pespire at 7 A. M. on November 13th, and arrived at San Lorenzo in four and a half hours. A boat for which we had telegraphed to Amapala arrived during the night, and at daylight we started for that place. Unfortunately, the tide being low, we ran aground on an enormous shoal of sand, and the tide continued to fall so rapidly that we were unable to get afloat. A large cargo boat having succeeded in keeping the channel, came within range. We hailed her, received permission to embark, and walking some distance upon the nearly dry sand, were then carried on board on the shoulders of the crew. The boat was taking ox hides to Amapala. Presently the wind died out, the men got exhausted with rowing, and we halted for two hours' rest on one of the small islands that lie between Tigre and Sacate Grande. While the men were rowing, each with a broad fan-shaped slab of mahogany fastened to the end of a long pole, I noticed that they rose at each stroke, so as to impress their full weight upon the oars in pulling back; also that they alternated twenty short quick strokes with half as many long slow ones. Our intended rest of two hours lengthened into five, it being necessary to wait for the tide to turn. But, even after we did start, the wind, which had been favorable, died out, and rowing had to be resorted to again. This was when we were half-way to

Amapala, which, however, we finally reached at 3.30 P. M., on the afternoon of November 14th. We thus terminated a somewhat disagreeable journey, during which we had passed forty-eight hours with nothing to eat excepting two meals of tortillas, or corn cakes, and fried eggs; and not enough of these. However, travelers can not be choosers.

We spent the next two days in waiting for an opportunity to get to La Libertad, Salvador, and finally left in a steamer of the Pacific Mail Line, at eleven in the morning of the 17th, going by way of La Union. Crossing the Gulf of Fonseca and threading the narrow strait between Punta Sacate and the promontory that holds the volcano of Conchagua, we entered the large and deep bay of La Union, and anchored about a mile distant from the town of that name. On the slope of Conchagua appeared the dome of the church of La Union. The thickness of the vegetation concealed the town. Several lighters were anchored off the shore, and came out to get some of our freight. At dusk we started for La Libertad, passing Conchagua, of whose beautifully green trees and cleared patches of pasture, beans, and maize we took a last farewell. Gliding by Conchaguita Island, we rounded the Punta de Amapala, and sailed about due west for La Libertad.

4. SALVADOR.

At daylight we were running directly in toward the shore. A high and very rough range of green hills extended nearly down to the sea. To the southeast were half a dozen irregular and broken craters, one of them dark blue and quite high. The most easterly was San Miguel. Just at the water's edge stood La Libertad, on a narrow and level expanse. A long iron pier projected into the sea, with a large wood and iron shed at the extremity. Behind the red roofs of the houses, above many of which rose flagstaffs, shone the green of the steep hills. The short mountain range beyond revealed one peak running to an exceptionally sharp point. A part of the range was covered with forest, and the clearings showed pasture land and plantations yielding beans, maize, and sugar-cane. To the eastward of this lovely peak stands the city of San Salvador. And I will seize the opportunity of stating here, what I think I have mentioned before, that it is the state only which is called Salvador, the name San Salvador being reserved for the capital. The misapprehension upon the point is general, and is sustained by the inaccurate nomenclature of atlases. As we neared La Libertad the vegetation displayed cocoanut-palms, bananas, and bread-fruit. When we anchored immense lighters came out and landed us, our luggage, and the freight. From the iron pier the heavy swell of the sea became more evident. The breakers dashed with a

7

noise like thunder, and seemed to shake the sandy beach
wherewith all this part of Salvador is bordered. The
steam cranes on the pier were used for raising and low-
ering passengers as well as freight, so rough is the sea
and so high above its surface is the pier. A large iron
cage, with a circular seat in its center, capable of holding
four persons, is lowered to the boat, and passengers are
thus gently wafted above the boiling surge to safety on
the pier. Hand-cars are run thence to the custom-house,
where the inspection caused us no trouble or delay. A
small covered stage, with five horses—or sometimes mules
—plies between that point and the capital. Formerly it
ran every day, carrying the mail, but now the mail is
carried afoot, and the diligence goes only when needed
by passengers. There being only one stage, you may
have to wait its arrival from the other end of the route.
Mules are always to be had—or to be waited for until
they arrive from the interior—and as the coach takes
eight hours in traversing twenty-five miles, we concluded
to wait for mules, in order to see the country better, go
faster, and be more comfortable. Pending their arrival
we inspected La Libertad. We had come twenty-one
miles from Amapala to La Union, and one hundred and
four miles from La Union to our present resting-place.
The latter does not need any detailed description. The
harbor is entirely unprotected, as open as the Pacific itself. The Government charges each passenger twenty-
five cents for landing on the pier, including the ascent by
cage. Packages of ordinary size are charged fifty cents

apiece. The national colors flying above the custom-house were similar in arrangement and outline to those of the United States, the stripes being blue and white alternately, the stars small and white, and the field in the upper corner, near the flagstaff, scarlet.

The heavy portion of our baggage had been sent forward in a cart, and was expected to reach San Salvador not later than six hours after ourselves. At two in the morning our mules arrived at La Libertad. They included one which was to carry both our light baggage and our servant, and we started at once for the capital, the bright stars and flaming constellations making our way clear. Behind us was the Southern Cross, before us the Great Bear. There was no moon. At first we followed the coast to the eastward, but soon left behind the damp hot air of the ocean, and ascended into a cooler and more refreshing atmosphere. Not until after many hours did we cease to hear the heavy booming of the surf. The road was crooked, rough, and rocky, but it was wide and of an easy grade. The only evidence of habitation was the surly barking of a cur or the shrill crowing of a cock. We met several other travelers; for, to avoid the heat, glare, and possible heavy showers of midday and afternoon, most journeying is done at night. Several times we passed ox trains encamped at the roadside, and with the first streaks of dawn others began moving. These were large skin-covered carts, drawn by two yoke of oxen, going to La Libertad to bring up freight from the steamers. Dawn showed a hilly and broken country. The general absence of timber and frequency of cultivation betokened a more thickly settled region. First we passed by fields of sugar-cane, beans, and maize, and then, as we got higher, we rode through miles and miles of coffee. Hill and dale abounded upon every side. Behind us were magnificent stretches of ocean; before us was the peak of San Salvador. Upon starting the houses we saw were of straw and thatched roofs; now we encountered the more pretentious mud fabrics, roofed with tile. There was only one town upon the road between La Libertad and San Salvador, namely, Zaragosa, with its single long, paved street, lined with orange trees. We stopped at the hotel there for half an hour to take coffee and bread. Then we crossed the crest of the mountain range through a narrow wooded cañon which gave passage to a small stream flowing into the Atlantic. The road from here on was wide and smooth. We met many people, among them some gentlemen in a mediæval-looking carriage to which three mules were harnessed abreast. Mule-back, however, is the favorite means of travel. Leaving the long and narrow defile of which I have just spoken we entered a beautiful valley, and saw directly in front of us the short range of hills at the extremity of which is the volcanic peak of San Salvador, its sides covered with pasture lands and plantations hedged in with arborescent fences of living green. To the left lay the city of Santa Tecla, the second in population and importance. It is connected with the capital by a line of four-mule tramcars, which run four times daily, the distance being

A Salvador Belle.

green. Here the band plays, from seven to eight, two nights in the week, under a German leader, and everybody, high and low, promenades around and around, as though pedestrianism was heaven's first law. The park is supplied with settees of artificial stone, and near the band-stand are several movable kiosks furnished with awning-covered seats. Offenbach, Suppé, and Strauss are well interpreted, and the then popular Boulanger March was given with dash. The promenade crowd was exceedingly democratic, and good-nature was the soul of the universal chatter. Arrieros elbowed generals, and peons preceded ministers. Even the glowing heavens shared this democracy, for the small moon was thrust into insignificance by thousands of starry rivals. Through and around the park enervating perfumes stole through nodding palms to entice to languor the sparkling strains of opera-bouffe. A poet or an artist would have appreciated the spectacle, but it was not altogether lost upon the humble traveler.

San Salvador is, as I have said, situated in a beautiful valley embosomed in hills. The volcano of the same name rises to the north. Barren mountain ranges, with here and there a volcanic peak, rise in the far distance to the right. To the east is the sharp volcanic cone of San Vicente, eight thousand feet high, the loftiest in Salvador. Between San Vicente and the city, and only five miles distant, is Lake Ilopango, which unexpectedly gave birth to a volcano about eight years ago. To the south a mountain ridge interrupts a view of the Pacific, but is

pleasantly shrouded with pasture and produce. On the
west the valley extends in the direction of Santa Tecla.
The capital is not only beautiful, but its altitude and un-
constricted boundaries conspire with its drainage to render it healthy. The remote view from the top of the
bell-tower of the cathedral is of barren peaks; the near
view of glossy, rich, and deep-green vegetation in diversified patches separated by cactus hedges. Looking down
upon the city, it sparkles like an iridescent pearl, and
you do not realize that it contains twenty-five thousand
inhabitants. It is compactly built, however, and much
of it is concealed by trees. The two principal squares
are the beautiful little Central Park, described above,
and the Plaza de Armas. A third is Morazan Park, so
small as to be invisible from the campanile. The President's palace is a large white wooden house with a
lofty tower. On the west side of Central Park stands
the Capitol, containing the offices of the Government.
The front is porticoed. Some distance away is the very
pretty wooden façade of a little church. The barracks
are quadrangular and enormous, with round towers
at the corners. One story is the general height of the
dwellings. I have nowhere seen lower built edifices
save in Caracas, Venezuela, the history of both of these
places revealing the terrific character of the earthquakes
that have visited them. Most of the city is laid out at
right angles, and is roughly paved, the streets sloping
from both sides toward the center. The sidewalks are
of brick, and of the usual Spanish American narrowness.

They are well lighted with kerosene, and policed by two
hundred men and boys drilled and superintended by a
man from New York. Their uniform consists of linen
trousers, blue cloth jacket, and Panama hat. Each carries a long stout club, and wears upon his breast a number and a metallic star. The theatre, which faces Morazan Park, has a graceful façade and emblematic paintings
on the pediment. The interior is painted in white and
gold and much ornamented. Its other arrangements
are, in most respects, like those mentioned by me elsewhere. Every portion of this theatre, however, was made
in San Francisco, and the various sections were put together here. Each of the lower proscenium boxes is covered with a fine wire screen, and thus reserved for families
in mourning who may wish to attend the theatre unseen
by the audience. Each side of the orchestra stalls is
flanked by the cheapest seats in the house. Both these
features are unique. No performance happened to be
given while we were in San Salvador.

In Morazan Park is a colossal bronze statue of the patriot Morazan, made in Genoa, Italy. The massive pedestal is decorated with bronze tablets in high relief, illustrative of the hero's career; and at the angles are marble
figures emblematic of the other Central American States.
The city possesses a good club, to which foreigners and
visitors may be admitted, and at which they may be enter-
tained. The unfinished cathedral is very large and in the
form of a Greek cross, with narrow, elongated arms. It is
being built wholly by charity. The dome and the roof are

of corrugated galvanized iron, and the former resembles in outline that of our own Capitol at Washington. The frequent use of this material and of wood in both the public and the private houses of San Salvador distinguishes it from the other capitals and chief cities of Central America. Red tiles and gayly stuccoed walls are thus dispensed with, and a sort of storage-warehouse effect is too general. The façade of the cathedral is being made of iron in France. The columns, walls, ceilings, altars, confessionals, and, in fact, the entire interior of the great building are of red cedar. The floor alone is of laid stone, artificially tinted to resemble colored marble. The ornamentation is of carved red cedar which, when oiled and polished, will produce an effect at once simple and rich. It will be the only church in the New World of precisely this kind of material and decoration. I predict that it will also be one of the finest in the New World. Attached to the cathedral will be commodious two-story houses for the bishop and priests. Priests are not forbidden here, as they are in Mexico, to appear in the streets in the garb of their profession. But though ecclesiastically influential, they are not so politically.

The Palacio Nacional is two stories high, with three Greek-columned porticoes in front. It is a very large building, occupying the whole of a square. The outer windows have a little stained glass in their sashes. All the offices and rooms open upon the corridors of the court-yard. The imposing entrance is guarded all day by some twenty soldiers, who sit on benches and hold their rifles in their hands. Many of the lower rooms are applied to barrack purposes. In the floor above are the departmental offices, containing very little furniture, and that little exceedingly simple. The edifice, however, is one of the largest and best of its class in Central America. On the same street, to the north, are the university and the National Institute, large two-story buildings, filling an entire square. They are among the finest in San Salvador. Their fronts are of stucco and wood, their roofs of galvanized iron, the architecture being solid and substantial. The institute is a sort of high school, preparatory to the university. It has about two hundred male pupils, while the university has about half that number. The former contains an exhibition hall and study and recitation rooms. The chemical laboratory and the rooms for scientific instruments and zoölogical collections were of course not lavishly supplied, for they had only recently acquired such furnishing, as the director explained to me, but they promised well, though they should have borne the appearance of being more used. The university contains the national library, most of the books naturally being Spanish, richly bound and kept in cedar cases with glass doors. Theological books appeared to predominate, though science, law, and history had their separate sections. The other collections of the university were beneath criticism.

The market is too small for the needs of the place. Its sections were made of iron in England. It monopolizes a block not far from the cathedral. The floor is of cement, well-drained. Outside the market proper is an open annex where the poorer women exhibit their wares, shaded from the sun by straw mats. The regular market was equally packed with things to sell and persons to sell them. The majority of the latter were either Indians or presented features of strongly marked Indian descent. Nowhere else did I ever see so vast a quantity and variety of articles brought together within the same space. Turning from the market, a very extraordinary sight is the President's palace, situated at an angle of the Plaza de Armas. Two sides of this plaza are lined with portales, or small shops opening upon a corridored sidewalk. The vast incomplete cathedral occupies another side, and the Municipalidad, or City Hall, the fourth side. Now, fancy, obtruding itself amid this scene, a large, wide, two-story wooden house with a three-story square tower and an iron roof, exactly such as may be seen in any large New England town, and you can picture the incongruity. I never saw it equaled elsewhere in Central America. But I ought to have been prepared for anything after having observed a sign which read, " Vaccination Office and Botanical Garden." When I entered and inquired there, I was relieved to find that the double duty required two persons. The lower story of the President's palace is occupied by guards and military officers, the upper by His Excellency and family. The house is surrounded by a small fringe of shrubs and flowers, shut in by an iron fence. The edifice, being of wood, might withstand an earthquake shock, were it not two lofty stories in height. It was planned by an American architect and erected by American workmen.

The cemetery lies a little out of town, to the west, and looking from it you get a view of the crater and the sharp peak of San Salvador. Just outside the gateway stands in solitary magnificence an enormous tree—a ceiba—twenty-five feet in diameter at its base and one hundred and fifty feet high. It stands walled in, as though to defend so august a prisoner from the touch of the profane. The limbs have been removed from the lower portion, but the massive head remains unscathed. In the cemetery earth or vault burials are exclusively used, owing to the destructiveness of earthquakes, in preference to the mural mode popular elsewhere. Some of the marble monuments were made in Italy. One of the most noticeable is that of a former President, who was shot underneath the great tree by an opposing political faction. As I was returning from the cemetery I met the funeral procession of a baby accompanied by a small brass band. This custom is observed by the lower class only, a band never being employed at the funeral of an adult in the upper classes unless he was a soldier. The procession was on foot, and consisted of the male friends of the bereaved family. The white casket, covered with flowers, was carried on the shoulders of four laughing boys. The men held bouquets, and walked hand in hand fraternally. Some of them were a little the worse for aguardiente, and the display had some of the features of an Irish wake.

About fifteen hundred troops were stationed in the various barracks. Drills and parades take place morning and afternoon in the sandy Plaza de Armas. The fine military band, however, discourses only on Sundays, Thursdays, and feast days. A painful sight in the streets was a gang of prisoners chained in couples, at the ankles, by huge iron links, the weight of the links being somewhat lightened by a leather strap attached to the waist belt. These convicts were on their way to one of the public works, where they were employed, and were escorted by a strong guard of soldiers, commanded by an officer.

Every house and store is connected with a court-yard, in or near which are often kept the horses and mules belonging to the proprietor. It frequently happens that this court-yard can be reached only by passing through the front door of the shop or dwelling. One day I saw a boy lead a mule from the street into a shop, and so on behind the counter through the back door into the court-yard. Foreigners alone are conscious of the absurdity of such a spectacle. Paper money is employed in Salvador. The bills are badly and cheaply made in London in imitation of the excellent ones produced by the American Bank-Note Company of New York.

The frequent and simultaneous explosion of a number of rockets merely means—not an incipient revolution, as might naturally be suspected—but a diversion of some kind, public or private, civic, ecclesiastical, or military. The Church and the theatre use up a great many rockets.

The theatre announces its performances by this means, and the Church thus celebrates its innumerable *fiestas*. Private families similarly commemorate a wedding, a christening, or a birthday party. A circle of convivial young men at a club or hotel indulge in the same sport in the back yard. These displays take place during the day, so that these curious people care nothing for the beauty and brilliancy of pyrotechnics by night. The noise alone seems to gratify them. The diurnal fireworks of Japan give pleasure because of being so constructed that the smoke generated indicates their varied movements in the air. This advantage—such as it is—does not characterize the rockets of San Salvador.

When I told a native gentleman at the hotel that my object in going to San Salvador was merely to see the place and the people, he said he feared that I would have to get a special permit from the President to inspect the barracks and other army quarters, if, indeed, any stranger could be allowed such a privilege. This serves to illustrate the conspicuousness that war and fighting hold in the eyes of Salvadorians. I much surprised my informant by telling him that the army interested me less than anything else. Revolutions and insurrections have demoralized the Government. A professor in the military school called upon a merchant at the hotel to make a purchase amounting to four dollars and a half, but before doing so he was obliged to notify the authorities, inasmuch as if the Government declined to pay he himself would be unable to do so, being too poor.

8

We did not omit to take the tramway to Santa Tecla, about twelve miles distant. The gauge of the road was great and the rails light. There were no cuttings or fillings worth mention. The cars were made by John Stephenson & Co., New York. Four mules were used to each car. Besides the driver was a conductor, who sold tickets and tended brake. The road leads through jungle and coffee land and passes by a station that is half-way between the two cities. At this station the cars going in opposite directions exchange their mules. The twelve miles are covered in about an hour and a quarter. Santa Tecla has a large grass-grown crater just behind it. The town itself is widely extended, with broad streets and large plazas and parks. The Central Park is a wilderness of shrubs and flowers. I noticed several very fine large private residences, with splendid woodwork to their rich dark verandas, windows, and doors, and having pretty gardens and fountains before them. In one of the sandy plazas a cheap market was in progress. The usual barracks and municipal buildings put in their plea for notice, and from every part of the town you could see the huge crater looming up, like an overhanging phantom, its impending mouth threatening the beautiful meadows that blossomed near. Santa Tecla seems to have been built more with an eye than San Salvador to earthquake shocks. The ground is not thought to be very solid, but there is enough street room to shield from falling houses. The tramway sometimes runs for long distances quite in the shade, almost concealed by cocoanut-palms, bananas,

Inner Court of Private Residence.

mangoes, and enormous flowering shrubs. Then, again, it passes between two dark walls of coffee bushes laden at that season (November) with berries which seem heavy with their dusky red. A diligence runs daily between Santa Tecla and the capital, and seems more popular than the swifter, smoother, and more commodious tramway. Old customs die hard in Central America. There are many good roads in the interior of Salvador, and diligences run daily. One runs from the capital to a town beyond Lake Ilopango, and communicates with a mule track three miles long, whereby you may reach the village of Ilopango, on the shores of the lake. The latter is about ten miles long from east to west, and five from north to south, and is very deep. In its center are the rocky remains of the extinct volcano to which I have heretofore referred.

At two o'clock on the morning of November 26th we were treated to a genuine sensation. This was neither more nor less than a heavy earthquake shock. I was suddenly awakened from a sound sleep, and as I arose the house seemed to be rocking from side to side. I heard the mice scampering from the roof, and dust and dirt fell in a shower from the ceiling. I lit my candle and found that it was exactly two. I looked out into the street, wondering whether it would not be safer to go there, and as I looked lights appeared in all the neighboring houses, and heads were thrust from the doors, as though my own fears were shared by the entire population. The rocking motion was like that which one feels in a small boat at sea. Three distinct earth waves seemed almost instantly to pass. The duration could not have been more than five seconds. The general direction was from south to north. A slightly vertical motion had been given to the bed which I had just vacated. Had the oscillations been a little stronger, or a little larger, the effect of seasickness would have been produced. Fortunately no more shocks came, but the city had become sufficiently awake. I returned to bed and slept till four, when I arose and, with my comrade, took a carriage for La Libertad.

These carriages are small and covered. They are propelled on stout wheels and stout axles, suitable for the rough, rocky road. They may be hired in limited numbers from the man who supplies the diligence. Three mules are used, the middle one being confined in the shafts. We reached La Libertad in six hours, arriving in time for the midday breakfast. At both Zaragosa and La Libertad the shock was distinctly felt and regarded as severe. At the last-mentioned place we had nothing to do but to await the arrival of the Pacific mail steamer which was to take us to Acajutla and San José. She did not arrive until the evening of November 28th, and at nine the next morning we were put into the iron cage, like prisoners of state, and safely embarked. The steamer took on eighty tons of freight, and then we set sail for Acajutla, saluting the receding shore and the neighboring Spanish steamer with three whistles and the dipping of our ensign. Two small German brigs which we had noticed while in port had spread canvas for fatherland the night before—a voyage of five months!

We followed the coast to the westward, two or three miles distant. It did not present many indentations. It was low and woody in the foreground, hilly, and even mountainous in the distance. A few small rivers here enter the ocean. Evidences of human habitations were sparse. We passed the boundaries of the department (or county) of San Salvador, and reached those of Sonsonate. Here we had a fine view of the great volcano of Izalco, smooth and wholly bare, like Momotombo, possessing a sharp, sandy cone, and noted for its great flow of lava. This enormous yellow outpouring had covered the whole summit of the volcano, and submerged the forests on its base with far extending branches like frozen rivers. West of this volcano we could just discern a few of the larger buildings of the city of Sonsonate. Thence a railway extends to the sea-coast and Acajutla, abreast of which, in the open roadstead, we anchored for the night. Acajutla, from that point of view, did not appear to special advantage. A high iron pier, covered with a shed, projected from the bluff, which was wave-worn into numerous caverns, great and small. The country showed plenty of forest land, and the hills behind revealed rich pastures and the usual crops of sugar-cane, beans, and maize. The distance between La Libertad and Acajutla is only thirty-eight miles, and the coast is named Costa del Balsamo, because it was thought that that medicinal plant was to be found only there. In the rear of Sonso-

nate is a range of volcanoes which reminds me somewhat
of Los Marabios in Nicaragua, excepting that here the
volcanoes are points in a continuous range rather than
isolated peaks.   There are seven of these outlying craters,
and two more nearer the coast.   That at the southern end
is the celebrated Izalco.

The slopes of all these volcanoes are deeply furrowed,
and their soil, excepting that of Izalco, is extremely fertile.   As we dropped anchor I caught a brief view of several lofty and sharp peaks in the neighboring republic of
Guatemala, the principal port of which, San José, is only
sixty miles from Acajutla.   There being a full moon, we
unloaded cargo until nearly midnight, and completed the
task at midday on the 30th.   At 1 P. M. on that date
we left for San José.   The range of rough, jagged mountains continued, parallel with, but at some distance from
the coast.   The level foreground was garmented with
both forest and pasture land.   One lofty volcanic peak,
named Mita, towered near the boundary line between Salvador and Guatemala.   A small river emptying into the
Pacific divides these republics.

5. GUATEMALA

Views of the splendid peaks of the famous volcanoes
Agua and Fuego burst upon us as we proceeded along
Guatemala's shore.   Agua impresses one by its height and

regular cone shape. Fuego boasts two peaks, the higher
one only being active. Companion peaks shot up in
rivalry, and notched ranges were scattered like gigantic
fangs, piercing the air at intervals. These pinnacles
punctuate with exclamation points the distance between
San José and the capital of Guatemala, and their smooth
slopes are rich in cultivation. At about half-past eight
in the evening we anchored in the very exposed roadstead
of San José. The lights of the Government and railway
buildings and hotels extended for quite a distance along
the coast. A pier ran out into the sea. A heavy swell
prevailed, and the breakers were loud in their reverber-
ation. The captain of the port came on board, wearing a
gold-embroidered blue coat and gold-striped red trousers
which would have done justice to a French general of
artillery.

Early in the morning (December 1) we obtained our
first view of San José. To the west was the cone of Atit-
lan, almost directly in front of the smoking and steaming
Fuego. To the right of this, twenty miles distant, arose
majestically the smooth, verdurous cone of Agua, and to
the east of this the smaller but sharp cone of Pacaya.
Behind Fuego was Acatenango, the highest extinct volcano in Central America, being 13,612 feet above the
level of the sea. Presently the great freight launches
came alongside of us, and all the passengers were lowered
in a chair. This method of landing passengers, swinging
them in mid-air over a boiling sea, looks more dangerous
than it is. You are fastened securely upon the chair,

and especial pains are taken to assure women and children. Our luggage had also to be lowered, piece by piece, and this took so much time that we should have lost the train for the city of Guatemala had it not waited for us beyond schedule time. On the pier were some policemen, whose uniform, including even the caps, was the exact counterpart of that worn by the New York city police. Club and star, coat and cap, almost persuaded me that I had landed on a wharf in North River. But the swarthy complexion of these civic guardians, the intense heat of the place, and the reality of the "cage" from which I had just emerged soon brought me to my proper bearings. The chief of the Guatemala police is an ex-policeman of New York. He has drilled his force into good condition. The pier was supplied with a track and traversed by a diminutive locomotive. Every passenger carrying baggage weighing more than one hundred pounds was charged one cent and a half per pound for the excess. Besides this a personal tax of two dollars was mulcted. This is inflicted by a company, not by the Government. If a person carries much baggage, the charge becomes so expensive as to amount to a duty. The railway station, custom-house, post-office, and hotel are at the land extremity of the pier. Raised upon iron or wooden poles, they extend along the beach, which is separated from *terra firma* by a sort of morass, thus making San José almost an island. On the other side of the morass is a wretched little village of straw and bamboo huts. This constitutes the seaport of Guatemala city. The railway station is a large structure of wood and iron. Here you pay six dollars for a first-class ticket (there are three classes) to the capital, seventy-two miles distant. The railroad is narrow gauge and the rolling stock of American style and manufacture. The road has been open about five years, before which time the trip had to be made by diligence, and occupied a whole day. There is but one through passenger train each way daily, and five hours are needed for the transit.

The first half of the road crosses a level plain, extending almost due north to the town of Escuintla. This takes you through a tangled forest, in which the most noticeable trees are ceibas of enormous size. The country is very thinly settled. At Escuintla, the capital of the department of the same name, we drew up inside a large wood and iron station, and halted three quarters of an hour for breakfast, which we ate in an open veranda beside the track. A bar was here discovered, presided over by a woman. Ere reaching Escuintla, the forest had begun to give way to pasture, and upon leaving that town we entered upon a district largely devoted to coffee and sugar-cane. Proceeding toward the capital in a north-easterly direction, we reached at last the mountain bases. Between the town of Escuintla and the village of Palin, a distance of but thirteen miles, the railroad rises over two thousand five hundred feet. The steepest grades are, I believe, four and a half per cent. The rise in altitude is physically perceived, and passengers close the car windows. We crossed eight deep and narrow gorges, over which wooden bridges had been built. These gorges looked as though they might have been formed during the great eruption of water from Agua, from whose flanks they are hollowed. At Palin we looked directly upon Fuego, bearing traces of scoriæ and lava. It was smoking gently enough just then, but bore evidence, in its jagged and broken summit, sand engirdled, of gigantic physical powers, when in other days, lava coursed down its sides into the forest. At Palin station a number of women of the Quiché tribe of Indians sold fruit, eggs, and cakes. These women were quite small in stature and revealed a Malay type of feature. Their hair was black, thick, and coarse, and was tied in a simple knot on top of the head. They were dressed alike in a coarse blue cloth, merely wrapped around the waist and descending to the ankles, one end being tucked within the other and thus held fast. They wore white jackets of coarse cotton, which did not quite reach the material that answered for skirt. One woman carried a baby in a fold of cloth strapped to her back. The wind at that time felt quite cold, but these barefooted, bareheaded, and otherwise scantily clad Indians were insensible to the chill. They had no vivacity or gayety, but preserved the serious and stolid expression peculiar to the Indian race.

A great deal of coffee and sugar-cane is grown about the base of Agua, and we perceived several large factories and haciendas. We made many of the sharp turns permitted only to narrow-guage railways, and several long "tacks," ascending as easily as a carriage would glide along an ordinary road. Splendid views stretched behind us and upon the ocean. Following a narrow, cultivated valley, we reached the town of Amatitlan, situated on the lake of the same name. This is a pretty little sheet, dark blue in color, of irregular form, long and slim, surrounded by low wooded hills. I noticed many boiling springs along the shore, as well as evidence of their presence in the waters of the lake itself, thus indicating the propinquity of subterranean fires. The local laundresses take advantage of this close proximity of hot and cold water. Many flocks of ducks disported themselves in the lake and added to its animation. Passing in several different directions, we came at last to a wide expanse in the valley. It reminded me of the great plain of Bogota in the Republic of Colombia. Soon we began to spy the towers of churches in the capital, but Guatemala can not be seen at a great distance from the windows of a railroad car, as so many cities can. A nearer approach took us past the elegant, new, two-story house of some rich citizen ; then a curious fortress threatened us from a neighboring hill ; next the walls of a huge penitentiary loomed up, followed by some workshops belonging to the railway company—and then our jaunt was over, and we alighted in a fine brick station. Here, for the moment, things wore quite a civilized look, though in a foreign style. A few officers stood about, in the uniform of the French army. The policemen, though badly sunburned, were evidently from New York. They wore the regulation club-you-if-you-look-at-me expression. Hacks, like those in New York, with more civil drivers than are to be found there, and with good horses and harness, stood ready. The waiting-rooms were ornamented with pictures of Coney Island excursion-boats and Broadway Insurance Companies. Small tram-cars, with conductors blowing whistles and ringing bells, started at regular intervals from the station door. A large closed mail-wagon, like those used in New York, and with two uniformed attendants, stood ready to receive the mail. I was dumbfounded, but soon recovered, having previously observed equally startling phenomena in unexpected places. It was too good to last. I knew that, sooner or later, I should find the aboriginal element cropping out through this modern gloss.

We entered a tram-car made in New York. By the by, the cars all had the official notices printed in English instead of Spanish. The badly paved street up which we rode was bordered with the customary one-story shops and dwelling houses, and gave us our first disillusionment. On alighting we had a few steps to walk to what is regarded as the first hotel in the city. It is kept by a German. It was a large two-story building with a courtyard laid out as a garden, and filled with orange trees, oleanders, orchids, ferns, vines, and flowers. A billiard room and a bar presented their usual attractions. The long corridors of the hotel were inclosed with glass; for Guatemala, being nearly five thousand feet above the sea, has a temperate climate, and the nights and early mornings are, in the winter (it was December), very cool.

The hotel was full, some foreign merchants and several members of the diplomatic corps living there permanently. Some singers in an Italian opera company helped to swell the list. In the evening we attended a performance of Fra Diavolo at the National Theatre, a large brick and stucco building, with a columned and pedimented front, like that of the Parthenon. The stucco is in blocks, in imitation of stone, is painted cream color, and, at night, looks like marble. The building is oblong, standing in the middle of a large square, and surrounded by orange and oleander trees, lawns, flowers, fountains, and walks. Huge iron gates are at the sides. In the pediment are the coat-of-arms of the republic and other ornaments in plaster relief. The evening was quite cool. People were wrapped in large old-fashioned cloaks, which recalled scenes in Quito and La Paz, as well as on the opera-bouffe stage—the conspirators chorus in La Fille de Madame Angot, for instance. Tall silk hats and gloves were worn, and canes were carried. Panama hats, however, were very common in conjunction with the enormous cloaks just mentioned. Policemen were grouped around the theatre doors. Electric lights dazzled the eyes outside the building and inside. For "grand opera" the prices were very moderate. We gave only ninety cents for our orchestra stalls. Exteriorly, theatres in Central America are not imposing; interiorly we found this one most commodious and sumptuous. There are three galleries and a parquette. The prevailing colors of the decorations are red and gold. The par-

quette has a brick floor, but padded benches. The boxes
are in the two lower tiers. The latter are shallow, however, and the boxes are not partitioned from each other.
The upper gallery was only a few feet from the ceiling,
and during the performance was fringed with a row of
heads Indian in type. The ladies presented all that
gayety and variety of toilet which I have already described as having witnessed in other Central American
cities. As a rule they were without hats, but wore feathers, which I did not think added to their beauty; neither
did the lavish use of powder and pigments, which the
electric light betrayed in the cruelest manner. Many of
the younger ladies, with their soft, olive-tinted skin,
glossy hair, and sparkling eyes, were very beautiful.
None of the men were in evening dress. Those in the
boxes wore "Prince Albert" coats, and those in the parquette exhibited all the colors and styles of a great tailor-
ing house. I noticed again the strange custom of the
auditorium's becoming filled at once and at the last moment ere the performance began, and of becoming entirely vacant during the long intermissions. Even the
ladies in the boxes stepped into the corridor, though
there was no room for promenading. Three proscenium
boxes were on each side of the stage, the lower one on the
right-hand side being reserved for the President and his
family. The stage was wide and deep and the scenery
fairly good. The orchestra numbered fifty and did
passably well. The principal singers were acceptable,
and so was the male portion of the chorus, or rather,

Coffee Picking in Guatemala.

I might say, the male chorus, since of the four women who appeared in it only one sang! The opera was followed by a ballet, which employed a premiere assoluta and a male assistant, and four secondas or coryphées. This ballet could not be taken seriously; but one is inclined to be gracious rather than critical when he gets a whole evening's entertainment for ninety cents. It was over by eleven. The opera has a subvention from the Government. During the winter it is given in either French or Italian three nights in the week.

On December 6th I ascended a little knoll in the northeastern part of the city for the purpose of obtaining a bird's-eye view which should suggest future peregrinations. A broad road, traversed by a tramway and lit at night by electricity, leads out to this knoll. A church, which is the oldest in the republic, covers its top. It is a small, narrow edifice, with a cylindrical roof, and contains some old carvings and pictures. In front of it is a tower, in the side of which is a recess containing plaster sculptures in high relief. Reaching the summit of the hill, called the Cerro del Carmen, I beheld the city of Guatemala at my feet. It is situated in a long, narrow valley, with a gentle and even slope toward the east, and is begirt with vegetable gardens and a few coffee plantations. Among the hills in sight were two, beautifully rounded, devoted to timber and pasture. To the west towered the great cone of the volcano known as Agua. To the left the sharp little cone of Pacaya peeped above a triple-peaked ridge. Far to the right smoked the crooked crag

of Fuego, with the extinct crater of Acatenango for neigh-
bor.   In the northern part of the city I discerned the
grand stand of the Hippodrome or race-course.   To the
east, upon a smooth low hill, were the white walls of the
fort of Matamoras.   As a contrast to all this the pink
walls and towers of the Castillo de San José gleamed upon
me from a high acclivity to the south.   From the Hippodrome to the Castillo the distance is two miles.   The city
itself extends no further than the Cerro del Carmen.   It
is compactly built and about a mile and a half square,
without including its southern suburbs.   The peaked
roofs are covered with brown tiles, and the vari-colored
walls spring from court-yards bunched with vivid foliage.
Then, again, the generality of the houses being of but one
story, the churches, convents, and public buildings, and
even the theatre, loom forth with picturesque prominence.
The cathedral stands in nearly the center of the city, and
with its dome, its towers, and its massive walls, makes an
imposing display.   To the north of it is the Church of
Santa Teresa whose walls and dome had been recently re-
paired, and now shone with dazzling whiteness.   The
massive church and old convent of San Francisco are half
way between the cathedral and the Castillo.   The convent
has been utilized for a post-office, and also accomodates a
section of the police.   Coming nearer El Carmen, you
perceive first the Church of La Merced, a very plain, low,
and massive structure.   Beyond it are the cream-colored
walls and red roof of the theatre, and further around, to
the left, is the old convent of Santo Domingo, which is

now occupied by the School of Engineers and Mechanics. Such are the principal points revealed by a *coup d'œil* of the capital.

The present population is said to be seventy thousand, but the valley contains ample room for a city three times as large. It might be seriously damaged by earthquake shocks, though these have not been frequent or heavy for many years, but it seems beyond range of the active Fuego. Good stage roads run in several directions into the interior. Coming down from the Cerro del Carmen, and strolling through the city, I observed that it was laid out at right angles, and that the streets were broad and the sidewalks particularly wide for a Spanish-American town. Paved with smooth flagstone, they were generally on a level with the roadway, which always inclined toward the center, in order to promote surface drainage. The roadway was badly paved with huge blocks and small cobble-stones alternately. One portion of this paving wore away or settled more quickly than the other, and the result was that the pavement was always rough. Occasionally the sidewalks were bordered with orange trees. Horse cars ran through the principal streets. The cars are small, with horse or mule teams, and barefoot boys frequently for conductors. The fare is five cents, and the voice of the bell-punch is heard, though I am not certain it is always punched in the presence of the passenger. Little paper tickets are given you, and, to insure your retaining them to the end of your trip, instead of throwing them away, as has been done, the management hit upon the ingenious plan of establishing a small lottery, of which among the tickets are the winning numbers. Hacks and public carriages abound. Those with two horses are two dollars per hour; with one horse, one dollar. The streets are arranged and numbered somewhat like those in New York, but still more like those in Buenos Ayres. A central point is chosen, the southwest corner of the Plaza de Armas, on which stand the National Palace and the cathedral. Avenues run north and south, streets east and west, both being numbered consecutively. Avenues north of the central point I have specified have the word "north" prefixed to their names; avenues running south of that point have the word "south" prefixed. The streets are designated as east or west of the avenue (called Sixth Avenue) which runs through the central point. Sixth Avenue, or Calle Real, is the chief business thoroughfare of the city. There are some minor streets generally named from some church or prominent public building situated upon them. Though the city is at present lighted by electricity, the old kerosene-lamp sconces have been allowed to remain attached to the walls. The stores and dwellings are but one story in height. They have large iron-grated windows and huge double doors of wood two or three inches thick and studded with big nails like the gates of a mediæval castle. A house located at the angle of a street will have its corner windows separated only by a slender stone pillar. This enlarges the outlook of the inmates, with whom peering and peeping into the street occupy a great deal of time. When a house has two stories, the upper one always has a neat little iron or wooden balcony to each window. There are some twenty churches in the city, and at six in the morning the din of the many-toned bells of different power awakes the people, and, continuing for an hour, prevents further sleep. But the bugle and drum calls are not nearly so frequent and enduring as in San Salvador and other Central American capitals. A few carriages course through the streets, and many horsemen, ox-carts, and mule trains. The Indians also compete with the beasts of burden. At the intersection of the principal streets you will always find these patient and industrious representatives of their race ready for any sort of porterage. For small packages they use an oblong framework, inclosed by rope network. This they bear on the back secured to their shoulders. They carry single large packages on the back, the strain being divided by means of ropes fastened to a stout piece of leather about the head. They generally travel at a fast trot. The weight of the burdens and the speed always surprise a stranger. So do the moderate charges. These Indians are great competitors of the ox-cart, and it is very curious to watch one of them trotting along the sidewalk with an enormous trunk upon his back. The market women, and people in a similar condition of life, carry everything upon the head. They also move along at a rapid pace. The Indians that abound in Guatemala are of very low stature, but stocky, and, of course, very tough. Three or four plazas invite attention. The prettiest is La Concordia, where the military band plays two or three evenings in the week. The shops are shallow and oblong, and contain a great variety of goods. The drug stores and book stores present an especially fine appearance. Many Germans and other foreigners are engaged in business here. Owing to the coolness of the climate, the shops do not open until eight o'clock, and the streets are never full of people before the middle of the day, while by nine in the evening they are quite deserted. Iron letter-boxes stand at many a street corner. The post-office, located in one of the many old monasteries confiscated by the late President Barrios, has a large tier of the most approved style of lock-boxes. The telephone abounds. The phonograph, when perfected, will find ready welcome. In these and other ways Guatemala shows her advancement, and merits the title of "little city of Mexico."

Though the capital possesses several forts and barracks, the military element is never obtrusive, and nothing seems to hint of a revolutionary spirit. About one thousand foreigners are found among the people. They are made welcome, and are neither hampered nor cajoled, as in some of the republics further south. Notwithstanding the cool temperature the native ladies do their shopping in slippers, and without their hats and cloaks, or at least with very thin shawls. The Indians dress in much coarser material, but quite as gayly, and, moreover, go barefoot.

Most of the public offices are grouped around the

Plaza de Armas. On the north side is the Municipalidad, or City Hall; on the south is a row of small shops, with the President's palace at the western angle; on the east are the cathedral and the archiepiscopal palace; and on the west are the National Palace and two of the barracks. On the south side the sidewalk passes under cover of the buildings there in the manner known in South and Central America as portales. The tramcars start from the plaza. Next to the President's palace are more barracks, and adjacent to the cathedral is the market. The southwestern corner is the central point for the nomenclature of the streets, previously mentioned. The Plaza de Armas is large, but not beautiful. In the center is a garden surrounded by a broad promenade. No large trees give shade, but the stone-bordered plots are filled with exquisite flowers and pretty plants with colored leaves. Many shrubs contrast with a few evergreens. Fountains disport in large stone basins, artificial grottoes surprise you, and the center of the plaza is occupied by a curious old square stone tower or temple, in which are the remains of an equestrian stone statue of Charles IV. The sculpturing is coarse and crude, however, like that in the angles of the temple. On the roof is a stand of four electric lights, which looks a little incongruous, but not more so than the barbed-iron fence by which the park is inclosed. The shops on the south side are but a single story high. So, indeed, are the National Palace and the City Hall. These have portales, with arched fronts and tile roofs. The Government offices demand no special mention, being plain and rather bare of furniture. The President's house is not exteriorly effective. It shares the general one-storiedness. A seated company of guards lines the entrance to the National Palace, and officers in blue coats and red trousers lounge about in every direction. The archiepiscopal palace adjoins the cathedral, and is one of the most presentable buildings in the city. Its gates exhibit a formidable array of brass knockers and locks, hinges and nails. The stone above is carved with the miter, keys, etc. The buildings surrounding the plaza have green, white, and drab-tinted walls, and pretty stucco ornaments in low relief.

The cathedral is very interesting. Together with the bishop's palace, it covers an entire block. It is approached by a terrace of rough, dark stone, on the edge of which stand four colossal figures of saints, who, I regret to say, have a very disreputable look. This arises from the coarseness of the stone and from the fact of their being battered and broken, as though by several first-class earthquakes. Several pillars with urns atop add a Roman effect. The façade of the cathedral is handsome and well proportioned. It is carved from a softish yellow stone. Two square towers arise. The segment which joins them contains a pediment, and this again includes a clock with bronze figures and hands. Of three huge doors only two, at the sides, are used. In the center are round pillars, and in a central alcove above one of the doors is a large alto-relievo figure of John the Baptist. The side walls have fluted columns attached.

The generally pleasing effect is enhanced by much ornamental carving. The towers are filled with bells, and the south one has, besides, a glass-faced Parisian clock. Inside the cathedral you are impressed with the excellent light, cleanliness, and good condition of everything. The great size of the church is at first unappreciated, because of four parallel rows of square pillars extending through its length to the grand altar, thus making five aisles, none of which are very wide, while the arched ceilings seem to lessen their extent. With the exception of the grand altar everything is simple. There are eight gilt side altars, filled with the usual assemblage of decorated wooden saints. Over the center aisle depends a row of crystal chandeliers containing candles. The ceiling is ornamented by strips of blue and white bunting, gold edged and star sprinkled. The pavement is stone. Against the pillars hang many paintings, some old, some modern. The stucco work upon the ceiling and the interior of the dome is good. The same is to be said of the medallions and scroll ornaments in pure white plaster. The grand altar beneath the dome is of white marble and gold, and all the accessories are either gold or silver. Near the altar is a seat of state for the bishop. At one side is a great pyramid of angels, surmounted by a figure of the Virgin. The wooden images are clad in gauze and gay-hued muslin, with silver-tinsel tiaras and long wings. The Virgin wears a fine velvet gown embroidered with gold thread. She stands upon a crescent moon. A near inspection of some apparently handsome columns in the altar showed them to be of wood covered with silver paper. The two arms of the cross-like cathedral were full of saints, pictures, and altars. Behind the high altar was the choir, and above the choir was a fine large organ, the gray metal pipes of which appeared to good effect behind the colors of the altar. The choir had seats of carved wood, with paintings behind them. The reading-desk was minutely inlaid with pearls in various intricate patterns. Upon it rested the huge vellum-bound Latin missal and music books. Service was in progress during my visit, but only a few poor Indian women were present.

The market, which occupies the adjoining square, has large gates at the sides and corners. The market women seemed to be either of pure Indian blood or something akin to it. Around both the exterior and interior were little shops full of alluring goods worthy of English or German importation. Other shops were devoted each to a special branch of domestic manufacture. The market was well supplied with running water, and its center was occupied by extensive sheds. Whenever the venders are exposed to the sun they spread small straw mats above their heads on poles. The vegetable produce, coming from two zones, was very profuse. It was in most cases heaped upon the flag pavement in a circle, in the midst of which squatted the seller. In one quarter I observed a large cooking-place where cheap meals were served to the poor people employed in and about the market. The Indian girls, though scantily, coarsely, and dirtily dressed, did not fail to wear finger-rings and gold chains.

Among the offices and shops in the same block with the City Hall, I found the "Administration of the Funeral Service," fastened to the walls whereof, by that irony of fate which is universal, was a bill-board of the theatre. What is called the New Cemetery—it is but seven years old—is situated at the southwestern angle of the capital, and about a mile from the center of the city. You can go half the distance by tramway. After that you have to walk, unless you take a carriage for the whole distance. You proceed by a broad, unpaved road, lined with the mud huts of the poorer classes. Leaving the fort of San José upon the left, you soon reach the cemetery's main entrance, simply, but gracefully built, with immense iron gates. Inside, to the right are rooms for the mourners, to the left are the rooms for the reception of dead bodies. Proceeding farther you encounter, to the left, a high, stuccoed wall, washed white; to the right, a row of mural sepulchres, six tiers in height, with a corridor and pleasing façade. The cemetery covers a large area of nearly level meadowland, whence you look up to the volcanoes Agua, Fuego, and Acatanengo. Owing to the slope of the city toward the east, only a few buildings and roofs appear. This graveyard is treeless save for cypresses. These are relieved by flowering shrubs. The broad, paved paths are at right angles. Fountains and large circular basins, surrounded by pretty flower-plots, stand at each corner of this necropolis, and also at the center and immediately within the gate. The pathways are lined with oblong vaults, monuments, temples, and cenotaphs, sometimes in Grecian or Gothic architecture, and of brick, stucco, or wood. A few are in marble, and many others have marble fronts. Those in wood or plaster are painted in weak imitation of marble, and have a cheap look. Sometimes the oblong monuments have bodies underneath them in layers, the mode adopted in the famous Père-la-Chaise. Sometimes bodies are kept above ground, and placed inside the monuments in tiers. Occasionally the tombs are open and contain little altars and an iron trap leading to the bodies below. These mortuary fabrics are usually placed very near each other and are not always separated by fences. The American plan of having large family plots, filled with trees, shrubs, and flowers, is unknown. A small and slender broken marble column was erected to the late General Barrios. It rose from a heap of rough marble rocks, the whole resting upon a great square, wooden cenotaph. The latter was painted to resemble marble—but it resembled nothing but painted wood. The six-tier tomb wall contained but few bodies—the fear of earthquake evidently rendering unpopular that form of sepulture. I was sure that this intuition was correct when I walked further into the cemetery, and, seeing a long, narrow, and very low building, entered it, and descended by a flight of stone steps at one end. These led me to a passage which terminated with a similar row of stone steps at the other end. The passage was lined with walls of tombs, five tiers each in height. I must have passed between many hundred niches, not one of which was vacant. The ends of several were sealed with slabs of black or white marble, on which were carved the name and death date of the occupant. The birth or age was very seldom given—a noticeable peculiarity of all Spanish-American cemeteries. Scripture texts, mottoes, sentiments, and so forth, are all omitted. As a general rule nothing is inscribed excepting the name, marked on the customary plaster by stencil plates. Another curious fact is that children and babies are not buried with adults. Near one end of the underground niches was a collection of miniature cenotaphs, monuments, and slabs, exactly imitating the larger ones in other places. This was the children's department! On the highest knoll of the cemetery was a lofty stone obelisk, erected by the country in memory of a popular general, named Zavala, who died a few years ago.

Returning to the city, I visited the pretty little plaza of Concordia. This is a park occupying an entire square, surrounded by a massive brick fence, and nobly stocked with palms, bananas, cacti, shrubs, flowers, and large trees. Irrigation is furnished by means of brick borders, so constructed as to hold water. Broad paths extend quite around the plaza, next to the wall, and here all the *beau monde* of Guatemala promenade when the band plays—in other words, on Wednesday and Saturday evenings, and on Sunday afternoons. The city possesses three good military bands—representing different battalions—and every night you may hear one of them, and frequently two, exerting themselves in melodious competition. One of them may be stationed in the plaza I have just been describing, and the other in the Plaza de Armas. The performance lasts only an hour, however. Four pieces are generally given—the lighter compositions of France and Germany usually having preference. National fandangoes and Mexican airs are also popular, and share in the applause and encores.

The water used by the inhabitants of Guatemala is brought by two aqueducts from different directions, tapping rivers at a distance of five or ten miles. Inside the city are twenty public reservoirs whence running water is drawn and where public washing is done. These reservoirs were built by President Barrios. They are made of brick, and some of them, circular in form, with steps, fountains, and pavilions, are ornamental as well as useful. Around the reservoirs small sinks, for laundry use, are made, and on the stone bottom of these buttons are too apt to be removed from resistless linen by infuriate washerwomen. "First come, first served" is the motto of the latter—generally Indians—at these little stone wash-tubs. Clothes are speedily dried by laying them on the grass. Large open-air swimming baths abound. There are also public bath houses with hot and cold water.

The Hippodrome is at a little distance from the extreme northern end of the city. Tramway rails have been laid to its gates, but the cars run there only when races are in progress. You can walk there on a broad, tree-lined avenue, which might almost be called an "alameda," between extensive meadows, and with only a few curious two-story houses on each side. These houses have wide piazzas all round their second story, and were built and rented by President Barrios as outlooks on race days. The Hippodrome is simply a half-mile racing track. This also was laid out and its circular music pavilion was built by Barrios. The grand stand contains a restaurant and a bar-room. The track is grass-grown, and is used only for running races. The views from the Hippodrome of the surrounding hills and volcanoes are very fine. At the opposite end of the city, near the railway station, is a goodly sized bull-ring, with low brick and plaster walls. Bull-fights are given there on the afternoons of Sundays and feast days, whenever the necessary chulos, picadors, and matadors are in town. At least one of these "seasons" is given here every year, a company coming from Spain for that purpose.

The general hospital is situated on the western edge of the city. It is a large building—one story, of course—well arranged and suitably equipped. Its good condition, its perfect cleanliness, and its many court-yards, smiling with flowers, are strikingly delightful to a stranger. A block distant is the substantial quadrangle of the medical school, with a large flower-garden along its eastern front, hedged in by a high iron fence.

The National Institute and the University of Guatemala stand pre-eminent in the educational system of Central America. The first is used as a preparatory school for the other. Both are under Government con-

trol. The charges are very moderate. The institute
has about forty professors and three hundred pupils;
the university about half these numbers, respectively.
The buildings occupy the whole of a large square, including the botanical and zoölogical gardens, which are
the institute's exclusive property. Both edifices are of
handsome stucco, with tinted walls, and the institute
has two stories, while the university has but one, besides
being very much smaller in other ways. A row of small
orange trees, next the sidewalk, entirely surrounds these
buildings. The institute is arranged in two large quad-
rangles; the university in one—much smaller. Both
the court-yards contain stone basins and pretty fountains. The lower story of the institute includes the
offices and apartments of the director and the study
and lecture rooms. The inner and smaller quadrangle
is devoted to the dormitories and dining-rooms. You
pass from the street through a fine bronze gate into
the large court-yard, the walls of whose corridors are
everywhere hung with maps; ethnographical, botanical,
and zoölogical plates; architectural types; and so forth—
an admirable means for keeping valuable subjects before
the eyes of the pupils. Up-stairs are more lecture rooms,
besides the library and the museum. The library does
not at present contain more than four thousand volumes. Several languages are represented, and ancient
and modern works are included. The museum is a
large room in which are various small collections of
curiosities and products of the country. A good assort-

ment of native birds are well mounted, but the nomenclature is not so good. Among the birds I observed a male and a female quetzal, the famous national emblem of Guatemala, always represented on a scroll inscribed with the date of Guatemala's independence, September 15, 1821. The two sexes are about the same size and color, save that the male has by far the longer tail. They resembled small parrots, and had very glossy green and yellow tails and black wings, with very bright crimson breasts. The collections of minerals and woods were small but representative. A case of Indian pottery, gods, ornaments, and so forth was especially interesting. The botanical and zoölogical gardens were both good, but, curiously enough, they are never open to the public, and their members are not marked, or in any way denoted. The zoölogical collection is varied, though small. There is accommodation for many more animals, but those on hand are not restricted to native specimens. There was no example of the quetzal, however, as this bird will not live in captivity. A large American grizzly bear presented himself. In the University building, besides the lecture rooms and examination hall, are the national library and its adjacent reading-rooms. The latter are provided with magazines and other periodicals of the day. The library occupies a large room, long, narrow, and high ceiled. It looks as though it might once have been a chapel. It is intended to have, around all the walls, three tiers of cases containing books, reached by stairs and galleries, but at present only three sides are filled. The librarian informed me that there were now in the library about forty-five thousand volumes, embracing, in many languages, general literature, classics, standard authorities, and books of the day, properly so called.

December 8th was the Church holy day of "La Concepcion," one of the two hundred festivals of the year. It is observed as a public holiday by everybody excepting Government officials. The churches were crowded with women. Men dressed in their finest filled the streets, the billiard-rooms, and the drinking-saloons. The festival was in reality announced at noon of the 7th by a most terrific clanging of all the church bells in the city. This din was repeated all the afternoon and half of the night. It was accompanied by a great deal of rocket-firing, and, as the rockets cost twenty cents apiece, their sale would seem to form a not unlucrative industry. At night the churches were decorated with flags and rows of colored lanterns. Grass was strewed upon the pavement before them, and special choral services were held. Almost every house bore candles upon its window-sills. The feast day of Guadelupe, an especially Indian *fête*, occurred a few days later. There are, as I have said, a score of churches in Guatemala, though Catholic churches in Central America, as well as elsewhere, are apt to repeat themselves to a great extent. The Church of San Francisco has high, massive white stucco and brick walls. The inside consists of one large nave with curved roof, and has a most neat and chaste appearance, being ornamented in gold and white, with black and white bunting displayed upon the ceiling.

The high altar is lavishly rich in gold and silver ornaments. The Church of Santo Domingo is of very peculiar architecture, the high and square façade being
supplied with neither pediment nor towers. The interior is exceedingly large and numerously provided with
side altars and paintings. The Virgin above the high
altar is magnificently dressed and covered with jewels.
From the terrace of this church you obtain glorious views
of the great volcanoes.

Before leaving Guatemala we made an excursion to
one of the old capitals, called Antigua Guatemala. Diligences take one there and also to Quezaltenango, the
second city in size and commercial importance in the republic. No other diligence roads run from the capital to
the interior, though there are plenty of mule trails. The
stages are all built on one model. They are long, narrow
boxes, holding six persons on their three transverse seats.
The driver occupies a high seat just in front of the roof
of the stage. Horses and mules are intermingled, and the
composite team of six is driven three abreast. Antigua
Guatemala is about twenty-five miles distant from the
capital in a southwest direction. The stage leaves Guatemala at 6 or 7 A. M. and calls at the residence of every
booked passenger. That is the reason that the moment
of departure is regulated by a sliding scale. We left the
city from the side of the fort of San José, and followed a
broad unpaved road between a double row of mud huts,
through long straggling suburbs. Indians met us going
toward the city at their accustomed jog-trot, and bearing
10

burdens for the metropolitan market. The men wore clean white suits. The women were in gayly colored frocks, and many of them had their babies slung upon their backs in shawls. The enormous loads which all bore excited my amazement. The men usually carried their burdens on their backs, the women on their heads. It consisted mainly of market produce in baskets. Some of these people looked bright and smiling, but most of them had a heavy, stupid expression, like beasts of burden.

Our road took us through vast corn fields. The fences were of bamboo, cactus, and ox-horn. Excellent views of Agua, Fuego, and Acatenango presented themselves, after we had mounted the hills commanding the city of Guatemala. We passed through the Indian village of Mixco, lying high up on the hills, with its church, plaza, and short, paved street. A ridge of hills now separated us from the valley of the capital. We passed many ox-carts, a few pack-trains, and still fewer native horsemen. Sometimes the road had been cut from a clayey hill-side, the ground having been comparatively soft at the time, but subsequently hardening. We proceeded through one or two mud villages, and threaded a long narrow gorge, in some places but little wider than the road, with steep wooded walls on each side. Coffee lands began to be visible. Agua was now quite near, and just before us smoked the chalky-topped Fuego. A little to the right rose the highest mountain in Central America, the extinct Acatenango. We stopped at a little place named San Rafael—merely a collection of huts—to take breakfast.

This is the regular breakfasting place where all stages halt, and four, owned by different persons, were there assembled, all bearing parties to Antigua, that being the chief point of transit from the capital. In a tidy little hut, surrounded by beautiful terraced flower gardens, we had found tables, on which a very good breakfast was served by Indian girls. While we were eating it we had plenty of time to admire the green hedges, the violet beds, the summer-houses, and the well-brushed paths. This meal renewed our vivacity and enabled us to reach Antigua about one o'clock in the afternoon, or about six hours after starting, including the pause for breakfast.

Upon entering Antigua we passed a neat stone fountain and basin and the ruins of a massive old church, and clattered up a roughly paved street to the best hotel. The town does not contain more than twenty thousand inhabitants, but it is greatly spread out, and covers the nearly level bottom of the valley, bounded by the slopes of the three great volcanoes. The churches and a few of the public buildings were destroyed by earthquakes over a hundred years ago. Before that time there was a still older capital about three miles south, situated between the volcanoes Agua and Fuego and named Ciudad Vieja. This was ruined by a great eruption of water from Agua. Then the people reared Antigua, and, upon this being destroyed, built the present capital, Guatemala, sometimes called Nueva Guatemala. Antigua is built at right angles and has the same general appearance as the capital. The plaza has, however, upon one side the Municipalidad and upon the opposite side the Palacio Nacional. The former is two stories in height and has stone columns in front. The very low and very massive stone walls and pillars of both these ancient buildings command attention. They, as well as the old churches, were built during the old Spanish rule, and still bear the carved arms of Leon and Castile—two castles and two lions rampant. In the city hall the troops on guard presented a most extraordinary appearance, their uniform being duck as to material and blood-red as to color. It called to mind both Mephistopheles and certain scenes in The Black Crook. On the eastern side of the plaza stood the old cathedral, whitened and in good repair, however, and with recent architectural additions. On the western side were shop-portales. I was sorry to see the square marred with many cheap and dilapidated huts and booths. They were used as shops, and as the city derived a considerable revenue from them it was easy to comprehend why such disfigurement was allowed. In strolling about the city one is apt to discover an old carved fountain or basin or portion of a building. The carving thereon may be rude, but it is expressive and interesting. Perhaps the chief interest, after all, lies in the old ruined churches and convents. These are all of stone, or, at least, faced with stone. Some of the walls, whether of brick or stone, show great durability, and the carving is commendable. Everything seemed to have been built with a view of resisting, instead of yielding to earthquake shocks. In no other seismic quarter have I ever seen such low and massive stone walls, such stumpy and gigantic pillars, such depressed domes, such flat arches. But even these could not withstand the earthquakes of 1773, which destroyed the city, together with eight thousand of its inhabitants. From the plaza a splendid view may be had of the volcanoes. Standing near the basin of the quaint old stone fountain I swept in all the environing country. In the marvelously clear air, Agua seemed near at hand, its sides covered with pasturage and beautiful plantations of coffee, corn, and beans. Agua may easily be ascended from this point. You start in the afternoon, sleep at a small Indian village about half-way up, and reach the summit early the following morning. On the top is an enormous crater. The neighboring active volcano of Fuego has never been ascended.

The ancient churches in this locality, as well as the modern churches, are recommended for their artistic work, and really the columns, friezes, pediments, and ornaments generally are very well worth notice. Among the ruins are to be found quite a number of churches divided, broken, hurled down, cracked, split, and scaled in the most extraordinary fashion. The two great " show sights " of the city are the Church of San Francisco and the Capucine nunnery. The former had a monastery connected with it, and was one of the largest edifices and institutions of the kind in all Central or South America. Not all of the walls remain, and there is very little besides; but in the general style of the architecture, in portions that remain of frescoed walls and stuccoed ceilings, with their religious and political insignia, coats-of-arms, and so forth, and in the many connected buildings whose original character can generally be inferred from their form, size, and arrangement, you see enough to realize the magnitude of the pile, as it once stood. In the remaining arches you always see large cracks at the outer angle, and when there are two stories the same kind of fissure extends from window to window. Enough columns remain for one to make his inferences. The domes and arches seem to have fared worst. Frequently, in making your investigations, you are surprised to see images of the saints still occupying their niches in the façade of some old church. In each of these wrecked edifices you will find an Indian family living, the members of which will serve as escorts and explain many things for a "*gratificacion.*" Altogether, Antigua is a dead city. The streets have no life. Except upon the plaza, no business is transacted, and even that is of very petty nature. Antigua is about one thousand feet above Nueva Guatemala, and is said to have a still more agreeable climate. It is not a little strange, however, that this climate, showing such great changes during the twenty-four hours—freezing at night and roasting at three in the afternoon—should be healthy; yet it is so for the natives, and it becomes so for foreigners after a little time; though at first one may be troubled with colds and rheumatisms.

In returning to the capital we took a road further to the south, which had a very long, steep hill. The method of going down these hills is not at all reassuring to the timid traveler. The stages are old and rickety, the tires being half off, and the wheels and springs so uncertain as to be bound with cord. The harness, moreover, was often re-enforced by string, and the brakes did not always act when called upon to do so. The declivity was not only steep and long, but also crooked and full of holes. Still there was nothing for it but to clatter down it at a frightful speed, coming to sudden halts now and then, to replace the harness, to tie up a chain with rope, or to lash a piece of wood between the break and the tire! The jolting was terrible, for the boy-drivers never select their road. The dust resembled that Egyptian darkness which could be felt. This of course prevented the views we had of the richly cultivated valley below us and of the distant city of Guatemala from being enjoyed in all their fullness. We halted at Bancena, a half-way station composed of mud-huts, for breakfast. On leaving we soon reached the valley, and passed a few plantations, the best of which seemed to extend toward the sea-coast. A good wide, hard, but dusty road took us the rest of the way to Guatemala, through a barren, brush-covered, uninviting country. We reached the hotel at noon, having occupied an hour less time than on our journey thence.

And now my charming companion and I had to part, he returning to New York by way of Panama and New Orleans, and I by way of San Francisco and New Orleans. At half-past seven, on the morning of December 13th, I left Guatemala by railway, and arrived at half-past one at San José. A Spanish steamer going south was in port, but not the Pacific Mail, though it was the day for its arrival. I put up at a ramshackle hotel, a very bad one, on the beach, not fifty feet from the surf, and spent the three succeeding days in waiting for the steamer which was to take me first to Acapulco, next to Mazatlan, and then to San Francisco. The noise of the surf was almost deafening. The breakers beat with terrible force upon the beach at high tide, and jar everything in the hotel, including one's self. The town is largely patronized as a sea-bathing resort. In the water the women wear old calico dresses; the men wear tights only. Evidently nothing similar to the Coney Island beach patrol obtains here. Though the swell is high and strong, the beach slopes very gradually and is exceedingly smooth. I left at three in the afternoon of the 16th for Champerico, seventy-six miles distant. The steamer was full of passengers, nearly all being bound for San Francisco. The low rate of the Pacific Mail Company, in competition with the transcontinental railways, caused a great flux of travel. The coast was low and wooded all the way to Champerico, with distant views of volcanic peaks, a scattered half-dozen of which extend to the westward of the great peaks of Acatenango, Agua, and Fuego. Agua towered high above the fleecy clouds, a splendid sight all the afternoon.

We reached Champerico about 9 P. M., a very good run. It has the same general appearance from the shore as San José, only the iron pier is much longer. It is more than half a mile in length! In the distant background there are no such splendid peaks as at San José, yet the volcanoes afford fine views. A narrow-gauge railway runs from Champerico to Retalhulen, the capital of the province of like name, about thirty miles distant. Quezaltenango is about the same distance off, and is also the capital of a province similarly named. It is reached by a stage which runs thrice each way weekly. We remained but a few hours at Champerico, and then left for our next stopping-place, Acapulco, in Mexico, five hundred and eighteen miles distant.

' The morning of December 17th showed me the distant mountain ranges of Soconusco, in the province of Chiapas, Mexico, and also distinctly informed me that my tour of two thousand miles, including ten weeks, in Central America, was an event of the past.

II

A RIVAL TO SOLOMON'S TEMPLE.

It is not a little singular that while so much time, labor, and life have been spent in exploring the secluded and savage parts of central Asia and Africa, more attention has not been bestowed upon the semi-civilized and easily accessible countries of Farther India. Until within a comparatively few years our knowledge of these countries might almost have been comprised in the words "Siamese Twins" and "Cochin-China Chanticleers." No book in any language gives anything like an adequate description of nature and man as found there to-day. The ethnology, philology, and archæology of these regions are scarcely better understood at present than they were in the remote era of Ptolemy the Greek geographer.

Probably few Americans are aware that since the exhumation of the buried cities of Assyria by Botta and Layard nothing has occurred so startling, or which has thrown so much light on Eastern art, as the discovery, about thirty years ago, of the ruined cities of Cambodia by Mouhot and Bastian—cities containing palaces and temples as splendid and stupendous as any in Egypt,

The Wonderful Buddhist Temple of Cambodia.

Greece, or Rome. Though historically these relics may not be of such importance to us as those of Nineveh and Babylon, yet, from an ethnological point of view, they scarcely admit of overestimation. It may be said that few countries present a more striking picture of lapse from the highest pinnacle of greatness to the last degree of insignificance and barbarism than Cambodia; nor is there a nation at the present day which can show so few traditions or produce so few clews to her ancient history. For beyond the half-fabulous records of the Chinese historians and a few legends which, it is to be feared, are more the invention of a subtle yet barbaric priesthood than an authentic narrative handed down from generation to generation, we have no account relative to this once powerful but now degraded country.

An ardent love of adventure and an enthusiastic desire to explore unknown countries impelled me to travel amid these unique regions. My tastes had already received the stimulus of partial gratification by two years of sojourn in Asia and the adjacent islands, when on the occasion of a third visit to Singapore in the month of December, 1871, I first heard detailed descriptions of the wonderful ruins in Cambodia. This determined me to extend my tour in that direction. Bangkok, in Siam, became the starting point, whence I proposed to journey entirely across the Indo-Chinese peninsula to Saigon, in Cochin-China. In these days of much travel and many books, it is hardly necessary to refer to well-known features of Singapore or Bangkok, which cities are connected by a semi-monthly line of steamers.

After seeing everything of interest in southern and western Siam, the proposed overland excursion to Cambodia claimed attention. I had invited an American missionary and our consul at Bangkok to accompany me. We thought a month only would be requisite to accomplish the entire journey to the ruined cities, whence my companions would return to Bangkok, while I should go on alone to Saigon. I spent much time in endeavoring to obtain a Cambodian interpreter, one speaking English or even Siamese, who was willing to accompany us, but met with no success. However, the missionary's servant was a Cambodian by birth, and, though he had passed nearly all his life in Siam, still remembered sufficient of his native tongue to be of considerable service to us. We took an assortment of medicines, especially a liberal supply of quinine, five grains of which were to be dissolved in our coffee regularly every morning. The offensive, and more especially the defensive, weapons of the party comprehended two revolvers and three large bowie-knives. We also carried a few scientific instruments, writing and drawing materials, and maps of the country (which, by the by, proved so incorrect as to be of scarcely any use to us); and, knowing that a *penchant* for accepting presents is not exclusively an American peculiarity, I also packed in my waterproof bag a few gifts for the King of Cambodia, the Governor of Siamrap, and some other great men. Provisions were taken in tin

cans. Money was carried in several small packages,
though our letters were quite adequate to secure us every
hospitality and attention. The letters were simply official
orders written in the vernacular idiom, with the great
seal of the Foreign Office attached, from the Siamese
Minister of Foreign Affairs to the governors of the provinces through which it would be necessary for us to pass.
To our passports chiefly we were indebted for the success
of the expedition. In Farther India, and, in fact, most
countries of the East, the natives humbly reverence authority and its enjoinments, and will readily find ways
and means of complying with a governmental order,
when the demands, bribes, or threats of an unknown,
unrecommended private traveler would avail nothing.
Upon the governors of provinces remote from the metropolis and the ruling monarchs we were dependent for
our means of transportation—elephants, horses, buffaloes,
carts, boats, servants, and guides—and everywhere on our
journey, when the passports were produced, we were
received with distinguished courtesy and consideration.
But I am anticipating.

Everything is ready and we are at last off. There
are three boats—two for the travelers and one for their
servants and provisions. The great floating city of
Bangkok, steeped in spectral moonlight and kaleido-
scoped with ten thousand colored lanterns, presents an
appearance at once weird and picturesque, as we swing
away from the consulate wharf, with our prows headed
up the whirling Menam. The boatmen break into wild,

rude songs, to which their dipping oars keep time; the distant howl of the pariah dog proclaims its quest of midnight prey; strains re-echo from many a Chinese booth, and the softening atmosphere improves them into a sweetness not their own; and so, standing upon deck, with night above us and mystery around, we wave adieu to Bangkok, that Venice of the East, and float onward toward the very heart of Cambodia—and our desire.

After a not uninteresting journey of two or three weeks, we arrived at Siamrap, which we found to be a town of about a thousand inhabitants, pleasantly situated upon the banks of a small river, four miles from the ruins at Angkor. Our letter from the Foreign Office at Bangkok being forwarded to the governor, was received with distinguished ceremony on a golden salver, and amid a conspicuous display of white umbrellas. Being presently invited to an interview, we entered the palace inclosure through an immense wooden gateway, preceded by the interpreter, and followed by all our servants. We marched fearlessly past the gaping mouth of a large iron cannon, for we knew no danger was to be apprehended, since its bore had been converted into a peaceful aviary — its throat of thunder into a throat of song. The governor received us in a long and broad veranda, and waved us graciously to some chairs, himself taking one opposite to us. Behind him, on the floor, were some red velvet cushions elegantly embroidered with gold thread, and facing these were placed the most magnificent betel boxes, cigar cases, and cuspidors we had as yet seen; they were made of pure Siamese gold and studded with costly gems. There was also a set of beautiful tea-things. Along the walls of the veranda were arranged rows of guns and swords. At the right were royal umbrellas, long state swords, a clock, and some glass candlesticks. The walls were hung with grotesque Chinese paintings. Grouped about the governor were a hundred or more prostrate officers and attendants. The rank of each might be divined by his dress, the material of which his betel boxes were manufactured, and his proximity to his lord and master. After conversing for some time, the governor ordered his band of fourteen instrumentalists to perform for our amusement. Cambodian music consists principally of noise — of the shrill and penetrating sounds produced by flageolets and other peculiarly formed reed instruments, and the banging, clanging, and rattling of tom-toms, cymbals, musical wheels, and bamboo sticks. All the musicians play their loudest, most interminable notes in full blast, at the same time, and for half an hour without intermission. The character of the music, however, is often sweet, sometimes wailing and rather dirge-like, although always played in quick time. The instruments themselves are capable of considerable melody if played with reference to tune and time, modulation and expression. While performing, the musicians sit upon the floor in rows, close together; there does not appear to be any particular leader.

The total distance we had traveled from Bangkok was about three hundred miles. The Governor of Siamrap having provided us with elephants, we started for the ruins of Angkor. We took but little baggage with us, being rather inpatient now that we were nearing the main object of the expedition, the *Ultima Thule* of our hopes. So passed we silently along until, in about an hour's time, emerging from the dense forest, we caught, as in a vision, a glimpse of that of which we had come in quest. A gigantic row of columned galleries cast its deep shadow to the edge of a sheet of water fringed with lotus plants, and, far beyond, three or four immense pagodas towered above glittering groves of cocoa and areca palms. The emotion awakened by these solemn and decaying monuments of a vanished race had indeed something of the bright unnaturalness of a dream. My heart was in my mouth as the Cambodian driver, turning toward the howdah, exclaimed with proud lips and flashing eyes, " *Nagkon Wat!* " for we were then at the very portals of the famous " city of monasteries," and not far distant was Angkor the Great!

And now, having arrived safely at the old capital, let us take a brief glance at the geography and what little is known of the history of Cambodia. When Angkor was at its height in the fourteenth century, Cambodia probably occupied nearly all of the Indo-Chinese peninsula. Native records indicate that the history of Cambodia commences about A. D. 200. We read of the army of seventy thousand war elephants, two hundred thousand horsemen, six hundred thousand foot soldiers, and incalculable treasures. Twenty kings are said to have paid tribute to it. At first the inhabitants led a roving life. They say they gave civilization to Siam, and we know Siam was for some time tributary to Cambodia. The name first occurs in Chinese history in A. D. 618, when it was a tributary of China in connection with all southeastern Asia. During the Tang dynasty Cambodia was a very flourishing state. The capital had twenty thousand houses, and many of the palaces were overlaid with gold and adorned with ivory. There were thirty cities, each with one thousand houses. It was the most civilized portion of the peninsula, and its riches became a proverb. About the year 1400 the Cambodians united with the Burmese to crush the Siamese, but the latter recovering themselves prepared to invade Cambodia, and after a terrible war succeeded in conquering the people—killing the king, destroying and mutilating the city of Angkor, and so devastating the country that it has never to this day recovered.

Even two hundred years ago Cambodia was thrice its present size; but now it is bounded on the north by Siam and the Laos States, on the west by Siam and the Gulf of Siam, on the south by French Cochin-China, and on the east by Annam and the Makong River. It is perhaps one hundred miles in diameter, and the bisection of the one hundred and fifth parallel of east longitude with the twelfth parallel of north latitude nearly indicates its center. Its population of about one million embraces—besides Cambodians proper—Chinese, Malays, Annamites,

11

and Siamese. The mineral, vegetable, and animal productions of Cambodia are varied and extensive. The chief articles of commerce are rice, tobacco, sugar, silk, cotton, and gamboge (a sweet-smelling resin); much fine timber, and several species of dyewoods, are also exported. The mountains contain gold, lead, zinc, copper, and iron. The animals are the elephant, tiger, leopard, bear, deer, buffalo, and hog; and the rivers are stocked with fish, some of them of immense size.

We, whose good fortune it is to live in the nineteenth century, are accustomed to boast of the perfection and pre-eminence of our modern civilization, of the grandeur of our attainments in science, art, literature, and what not, as compared with those whom we call ancients; but still we are compelled to admit that in many respects they have far excelled some of our recent endeavors, and notably in the fine arts of architecture and sculpture. In style and beauty of architecture, solidity of construction, and magnificent and elaborate sculpture, the great Nagkon Wat Temple of Buddha has no superior, nor any rival, standing at the present day. The first view of the ruins is almost overwhelming. Neither Thebes nor Memphis has anything so enigmatical to show. It is grander than anything left to us by Greece or Rome. At a first sight one is most impressed with the magnitude, minute detail, high finish, and elegant proportions of this temple, and then to the bewildered beholder arise mysterious afterthoughts—Who built it? When was it built? and Where now are the descendants of those who built it? It is doubtful if these questions will ever be satisfactorily answered. There exist no credible traditions—all is absurd fable or extravagant legend.

We entered first upon an immense causeway, the stairs of which were flanked with six huge griffins, each carved from a single block of stone. This causeway, which leads directly to the main entrance of the temple, is about eight hundred feet in length and thirty in width, and is paved with stones which measure four feet in length by two in breadth. On each side of it are artificial lakes, fed by springs, and each covering about five acres of ground. We passed through one of the side gates, and crossed the square to a bamboo shed, situated at the very entrance of the temple. Enbosomed in the midst of a perfect forest of cocoa, betel, and toddy palms, and with no village in sight—excepting a dozen or more huts, the abode of priests having charge of it—the general appearance of this wonderful temple is beautiful and romantic, as well as grand and impressive. A just idea of it can hardly be conveyed in words; it must be seen to be properly appreciated. Still, a detailed description will assist the imagination somewhat in forming a proper estimate of the grand genius which planned and the skill and patience which executed such a masterpiece of architecture.

The outer wall of Nagkon Wat—which words signify a city or assemblage of temples or monasteries—about half a mile square, is built of sandstone, with gateways upon each side, which are handsomely carved with figures of gods and dragons, arabesques, and intricate scrolls. Upon the western side is the main gateway, and passing through this and up a causeway paved with great slabs of stone, for a distance of a thousand feet, you arrive at the central main entrance of the temple. The foundations of Nagkon Wat are as much as ten feet in height, and are very massively built of a species of volcanic rock. Including the roof, the entire edifice—which is raised on three terraces, the one about thirty feet above the other— is of stone, but without cement, and so closely fitting are the joints as even now to be scarcely discernible. The shape of the building is oblong, being about eight hundred feet in length and six hundred feet in width, while the highest central pagoda rises some two hundred and fifty feet or more above the ground, and four others, at the angles of the inner court, are no less than one hundred and fifty feet each in height! The quarries where the stone, a fine-grained sandstone, was hewed, are about two days' travel, or thirty miles distant, and it is supposed the transportation of the immense bowlders could have been effected only by means of a water communication— a canal or river, or when the country was submerged at the end of the rainy season. In the stone pits may still be seen large blocks, partially separated from the parent rock, and bearing many marks of the quarrier's chisel.

Passing between low railings, we ascend a platform composed of slabs four feet in length, and enter the temple itself through a columned portico, the façade of which is beautifully carved in low relief with ancient mythological subjects and arabesques equaling those of Nineveh. From this doorway, on both sides, runs a corridor with a double row of columns cut, base and capital, from single blocks, with a double, oval, carved roof, and consecutive sculptures on the outer wall. This gallery of sculptures, which forms the exterior of the temple, consists of over half a mile of continuous pictures, cut in low relief, upon sandstone slabs six feet in width. The sculptures display a high degree of art and mechanical skill. Their subjects are chiefly taken from Hindoo mythology—from the Ramayana, the "Iliad of the East," the Sanskrit epic poem of India, with its twenty-five thousand verses describing the exploits of the god Rama and the son of the King of Oudh—which the builders of the temple either brought with them or received from India, or which was known by translations throughout Cambodia. The contests of the King of Ceylon and Hanuman, the Monkey-God, are also graphically represented. There is no keystone used in the arch of this corridor, but its ceiling is intricately carved. On the walls are sculptured the immense number of one hundred thousand separate figures! Entire scenes from the Ramayana are pictured; one, I remember, occupies two hundred and fifty feet of the wall. Weeks might be spent in studying, identifying, and classifying the varied subjects of this wondrous gallery. The pictures are very expressive and animated, the attitudes of the figures being natural and grouped with considerable skill. You may see warriors riding upon elephants and in chariots, foot soldiers with shield and spear, boats, unshapely divinities, trees, monkeys, tigers, griffins, hippopotami, serpents, fishes, crocodiles, bullocks, tortoises, men with beards, and helmeted soldiers of immense physical development. The figures stand somewhat like those on the great Egyptian monuments, the side partly turned toward the front. In the case of the men, one foot and leg are always placed in advance of the other. I noticed, besides, five horsemen, armed with spear and sword, riding abreast, like those which may be seen upon the Assyrian tablets of the British Museum.

In the processions several of the kings are preceded by musicians playing upon shells and long bamboo flutes. Some of the kings carry a sort of battle-axe, some a weapon which much resembles a golf-club, and others are represented as using the bow and arrow. In one place is a grotesque divinity who sits, elegantly dressed, upon a throne surmounted by umbrellas. This figure, of peculiar sanctity, evidently had been recently gilded, and before it, upon a small table, were a dozen or more josssticks, kept constantly burning by the faithful. But it is almost useless to particularize when the subjects and style of execution are so diverse. The most interesting sculptures are in two compartments, called by the natives respectively the procession and the three stages of heaven, earth, and hell. What gives a peculiar interest to this section is the fact that the artist has represented the different nationalities in all their distinctive characteristic features, from the flat-nosed savage in the tasseled garb of the Pnom and the short-haired Lao, to the straight-nosed Rajaput, with sword and shield, and the bearded Moor, giving a catalogue of nationalities, like another column of Trajan, in the predominant conformation of each race. On the whole, there is such a prevalence of Hellenic cast in the features and profiles, as well as in the elegant attitude of the horsemen, that one might suppose that Xenocrates of old, after finishing his labors in Bombay, had made an excursion to the East.

In some compartments are represented the delights of paradise, in others the punishments of the infernal regions. A crowd of persons are entering paradise and are received in palankeens; they have with them banners, fans, parasols and boxes for holding betel, without which even paradise would not be perfect happiness to a Cambodian. The elect, seated on a magnificent dais, are surrounded by a great number of women with caskets and fans in their hands, while the men are holding flowers and have children on their knees. These appear to be all the joys of paradise. The punishments of the infernal regions, on the contrary, are varied and numerous; and while the elect, who are enjoying themselves in glory, are all fat and plump, the poor condemned beings are so lean that their bones show through their skin, and the expression of their faces is pitiful and full of a most comic seriousness. Some are being pounded in mortars, while others hold them by the feet and hands; some are being sawed asunder; others are led along like buffaloes with ropes through their noses. In other places the executioners are cutting men to pieces

with sabers; while a crowd of poor wretches are being
transfixed by the tusks of elephants, or on the horns of the
rhinoceros.   Fabulous animals are busy devouring some;
others are in irons, and have had their eyes put out.   In
the center sits the judge with his ministers, saber in hand;
all the guilty are dragged before them by the hair or feet.
In the distance is visible a furnace and another crowd of
people under punishment, being tortured in diverse ways
—impaled, roasted on spits, tied to trees and pierced with
arrows, suspended with heavy weights attached to their
hands and feet, devoured by dogs or vultures, or crucified
with nails through their bodies.

There are figures sculptured in high relief and of
nearly life size upon the lower parts of the walls about
the entrance; all are females.   Their dresses are not the
same as those worn by the Cambodians of the present day.
The carving seems to have been done after the blocks
were placed in position.   The interior of the quadrangle,
bounded by the long corridor just described, is filled with
galleries or halls (formed with huge columns), which
cross one another at right angles.   In the Nagkon Wat
as many as fifteen hundred and thirty-two solid columns
have been counted, and among the entire ruins of Angkor
there are reported to be the immense number of six thousand, almost all of them monoliths and artistically carved!
On the inner side of the corridor are blank windows, each
of which contain seven beautifully turned little mullions.
At the time of my visit the ceilings of the galleries were
hung with tens of thousands of bats, while pigeons and

An Angle of the Great Court.

other birds had made themselves comfortable nests in out-of-the-way corners.

We mount steep staircases, with steps not more than four inches in width, to the center of the galleries, which here bisect one another. There are two detached buildings in this square, which, in all probability, were formerly used as image houses, and now contain Buddhas of recent date. In one of the galleries I saw two or three hundred images, made of stone, wood, brass, and clay, of all shapes, sizes, and ages. Joss-sticks were burning before the largest of them, which were daubed with red paint and partially gilded. We pass on across another causeway, with small image houses on each hand, and up a steep flight of steps, fully thirty feet in height, to other galleries crossing each other in the center, above which rises the grand central pagoda, two hundred and fifty feet in height. The four smaller ones which I have already mentioned are much dilapidated and do not now display their full height; the porticoes also bear evidence of the pressure of the heavy hand of time. Upon the four sides of the base of the highest spire are colossal images of Buddha. These figures are grandly placed, for when the doors of the inclosing rooms are opened, from their high position they overlook the surrounding country, and Cambodia is thus contemplated by her wondrous gods of stone. The priests of Nagkon Wat worship here at the present day. There is one more gallery, and then we come to the outer corridor and pass through a magnificent doorway to the rear of the temple and walk round to our camp, not knowing which to admire the more, the grand conception of the design or the mechanical skill of the performance.

Before I speak of the builders and age of the ruins of Angkor, reference should be made to the special religious worship to which Nagkon Wat was dedicated. It may be that the aboriginal inhabitants of the Indo-Chinese peninsula were snake worshipers, then Brahmans, and afterward Buddhists, as probably were the people of northern India before the arrival of the Aryans; but I must dissent from the view of Ferguson, the distinguished writer on architecture, that Nagkon Wat was dedicated to Naga, or serpent worship — to Phaya Naght, the snake god. There are representations of the snake god in several of the compartments of the grand gallery, and the roof, cornices, and balustrades are decorated with five, seven, and nine headed snakes, says Ferguson. True; but the last Buddha, Gaudama, was guarded in his youth, according to the Pali mythology, by a snake, which has ever since been honored and used in the ornamentation of Buddhist temples throughout Farther India. The word Naga is the name of a fabulous dragon in all languages of the East Indian Archipelago. In the Jaina temples the seven-headed snakes are the most prominent adornments. We would hardly be warranted in saying Nagkon Wat was of Brahmanical origin because the gate and many other parts of it are ornamented with Hindoo deities and female figures, for these are found in the Buddhist temples of China, Tartary, Siam, and Burmah. The Mohammedans have adopted and adapted much of the mythology of the Jews. In China, Buddhism is mixed up with Confucianism and Tauism, and in Cambodia with Brahmanism and Jainism.

All the evidence which I can obtain best supports the belief that Nagkon Wat was a Buddhist shrine. The combination of the four-faced Buddha occurs once in the great temple, and frequently among the ruins of Angkor. The female figures upon the lower parts of the wall, with their oblique eyes, flat noses, and thick lips, are evidently of Tartar origin, and from Thibet perhaps Buddhism came to central Indo-China. The inscriptions are in a corrupt form of the Buddhist sacred language. As far as we know, without relying upon native records, the people who have inhabited the country of Cambodia since about A. D. 1,000, at least three hundred years before the building of the temple, were Buddhists. I am inclined to think that the architecture of Nagkon Wat is symbolical of the Buddhist cosmology. The numbers three, seven, nine, and multiples of nine seem to be mystic and sacred numbers among the Buddhists. There are supposed to be seven circles of rock about Mount Meru, the center of the Buddhist universe, as there are seven circles on the central tower and seven mullions in the windows of Nagkon Wat. The sacred mount is supported on three platforms—so are there three terraces to this temple. Mount Meru rises from the ocean, and it seems to have been intended that Nagkon Wat, surrounded by its lakes and moats, should rise from a sort of inland sea. The temple of Boro-Buddor, in Java, has seven terraces. Some of the Buddhist temples which I have seen in Pekin, China, have three terraces and triple roofs. In Nagkon Wat there are three approaches, the gateways are three in number, and there are three ornaments on the brows of the female figures or angels. In China the priesthood are ordained upon a triple terrace of their monasteries. The first terrace is for Buddha, the second for the written law, and the third for the monastic community. And even supposing that the builders of Nagkon Wat came originally from Ceylon, where snake worship has always been in vogue (though the Singhalese have been Buddhists for at least two thousand years), I do not see why they may not have brought with them a species of Buddhism, debased or modified with Naga symbolism, as easily as one corrupted by Brahmanism.

And now let me approach the interesting subjects of the founders of Nagkon Wat and the date of its erection. Learned men who have visited the ruins have attempted to form opinions from studies of its construction, and especially its ornamentation. One would at first almost despair of reaching a decision or passing judgment when he saw in the same temple carved images of Buddha, four and even thirty-two armed, and two and sixteen-headed divinities, the Indian Vishnu, gods with wings, Burmese heads, snake gods, Tartar figures, representatives of the Ceylon mythology, etc., though, as already indicated, these facts in themselves would not prove insurmountable obstacles to a knowledge of the founders. The juxtaposition in one temple of the sym-

bols of so many different religions will not seem so
strange when we remember that one great faith of India,
namely, Vishnuism, appears to be a curious amalgamation
of serpent worship, Sivaism, Jainism, and Sabianism.
Some archæologists have supposed Nagkon Wat to be
fourteen hundred years old, to have been built by different kings, and to have been completed by one who was a
Buddhist. The Cambodians still possess accounts of the
introduction of Buddhism. The celebrated German Orientalist, Bastian, thinks this temple was built for the reception of the learned patriarch Buddhaghosa, who
brought the holy books of the Trai-Pidok from Ceylon.
And Bishop Pallegoix, a French Roman Catholic missionary who resided many years in Siam, refers its erection to the reign of Phra Pathum Suriving, at the time
the sacred books of the Buddhists were brought from
Ceylon, and Buddhism became the religion of the Cambodians. The natives themselves can throw no light upon
this subject. I asked one of them how long the temple
had been built. " None can tell—many hundred years
ago," he replied. I asked if the Cambodians or some
other race erected Nagkon Wat, and he answered frankly:
" I do not know; but it must either have sprung up from
the ground or been built by giants, or, perhaps, by the
angels." Another man said he did not believe it was
built by angels, for he could see the effect of the tools of
man upon it—certainly an amazing display of intellectual
acumen for a native. But still the Cambodians of the
present day, whose genius expresses itself only in the

carving of their boats, have no idea that their ancestors constructed these temples. It seems improbable that a race so poor, indolent, and ignorant as the present could ever have designed and made these splendid causeways and temples. Cambodians are fond of saying: "If man built the Nagkon Wat, it must have been built by a race of more power and skill than any to be found now."

But then, if it was some other, now extinct, race, who made these works, how comes it that they, with their superior energy, were swept away by the Laos and Siamese, timid tribes who really have no fight in them at all? And if we should rather credit the ancient Cambodians with the authorship of this temple, then the disappearance of a once splendid civilization and the relapse of a people into a primitiveness bordering, in some quarters, on the lower animals, seem to prove that man is a retrogressive as well as progressive being, and that he may probably relapse into the simpler forms of organic life from which he is supposed by some to have originally sprung. Then, also, we would naturally ask: Was civilization, in the complex meaning we give that word, in keeping among the ancient Cambodians with what such prodigies of architecture seem to indicate? The age of Phidias was that of Sophocles, Socrates, and Plato; Michael Angelo and Raphael succeeded Dante. There are luminous epochs during which the human mind, developing itself in every direction, triumphs in all, and creates masterpieces which spring from the same inspiration. Have the nations of India ever known such periods of special glory? It appears little probable, and it is only necessary to read the Chinese traveler of the thirteenth century whom the Emperor Ching-Tsung sent as an ambassador to Cambodia, and whose narrative the French Orientalist Rémusat has translated, to be convinced that it was never reached by the ancient Cambodians. He describes the monuments of the capital, most of which were covered with gilding, and he adds that, with the exception of the temples and the palace, all the houses were only thatched. Their size was regulated by the rank of the possessor, but the richest did not venture to build one like that of any of the great officers of state. Despotism induced corruption of manners, and some customs mentioned show actual barbarism.

M. Mouhot, a French naturalist, who gave the first exact account of these since celebrated ruins, was strongly of the opinion that they were built by some of the lost tribes of Israel. The idea is worthy of consideration, for there are several thousand Christians in Burmah whose doctrines agree perfectly with those of the Jews, who, it is well known, have penetrated into the remotest parts of Asia. M. Mouhot, in his travels through Indo-China, made many efforts to discover traces of Jewish emigration to Siam or Cambodia, but met with nothing satisfactory excepting a record of the "Judgment of Solomon"—attributed to one of their kings, who had become a god after having been, according to their ideas of metempsychosis, an ape, an elephant, etc. The record was found preserved in one of the Cambodian sacred books. Everywhere M. Mouhot was told there were no Jews in the country. Still he could not but be struck by the Hebrew character of the faces of many of the savage Stiens; and when looking at the figures in the bas-reliefs of Ångkor, he could not avoid remarking the strong resemblance of the faces there to those of these savages. Besides the similar regularity of features, they had the same long beards, straight waist-cloths, and also the same weapons and musical instruments. On the other hand, it would seem probable that if the temple had been built by one of the lost tribes of Israel, the Gothic architecture of the thirteenth century, rather than the orders of pagan Rome, would have been introduced. Probably the greater number of the figures in the bas-reliefs resemble the Cochin-Chinese more than any other neighboring race. It is M. Mouhot's belief that, without exaggeration, the antiquity of some of the oldest parts of Ångkor may be fixed at more than two thousand years, and that the age of the more recent portions approximates this period. But where are now the race of people who had the genius to plan, and the skill and patience to erect such magnificent structures? No trace of them exists among the Cambodians of the present day, or among the surrounding nations, unless, indeed, faith is to be placed in the statement concerning the Stiens and another race — the Bannans — who inhabit the old country of Tsiampa. If the savage Stiens, or their ancestors, were the builders of Nagkon Wat, historical proof of the fact might be excused in view of their total ignorance of the art of writing. Their spoken language contains many words like the Cambodian. Their traditions mention the deluge. Another circumstance of some interest is that the foundation of the neighboring city of Angkor is referred by the native historians to a prince of Roma, or Ruma, and that the name of Roma is familiar to nearly all the Cambodians, who place it at the western end of the world. The presence of Roman Doric pillars at Nagkon Wat might perhaps be mentioned in this connection.

Whether Nagkon Wat was built by some aborigines of the country, the ancestors of the present hill tribes, or whether the ancient Cambodians came from the northwest, from Tartary, and were simply a branch of the Siamese or Burmese race, has yet to be determined. If we assume that the Cambodians built the city of Angkor, it is still difficult to fix their origin. Their physiognomy, character, and religion would seem to bespeak a Thibetan or Tartar and Brahmanic descent; their stone buildings resemble those in India; their laws savor of China and Mencius; while their language is of Sanskrit and Chinese amalgamation. The Annamese, the neighbors of the Cambodians on the east, possess the manners, laws, written language, and customs of the Chinese, yet they are apparently a distinct race. When the Buddhists were driven out of India in the fourth century, some of them took refuge in Thibet, others in Ceylon. Afterward the former went to Cochin-China, while the latter crossed to Burmah and Cambodia. Those settling in Cambodia might have reared this vast temple, retaining, it is true, the myths of the old superstition, but commemorating their adoption of a better and purer faith. And if we agree that wars have driven the ancient Cambodians from their country, where are now their descendants? Perhaps in the adjoining provinces of Siam and Laos, where are to be found to-day districts whose population is almost entirely composed of Cambodians who were originally led away captive from their native country to people the "desert places" of the peninsula.

The general appearance of the buildings—the deeply worn stairs, the battered and decayed columns and slabs, the moss-covered and fallen roof, the absence of the key-stone in the arches—all betoken considerable age, giving evidence of another people and another civilization. The style of the architecture of the temple resembles both the temples of India and of Java, and this would, perhaps, seem to indicate a Hindoo or Malay origin. There is little resemblance to the Egyptian monuments. Here all is light, airy, graceful; there all is massive, severe, and grand. The architecture of Nagkon Wat, however, really follows no order recognized in the West. It is neither Egyptian, Assyrian, Greek, nor Saracenic, but rather, I should say, a combination of all. If we concur with the ethnologist Pickering in the belief that the Siamese were of Malay origin, then the question might arise, Did the same race who built the temple of Boro-Buddor in Java also build that of Nagkon Wat in Cambodia? They have, I know, a few resemblances. Boro-Buddor is a bell-shaped structure about one hundred feet in height and six hundred feet in diameter. It is built in seven galleries or terraces, without cement, and has four staircases which lead to its summit. The whole is intricately and beautifully carved. There are between five and six hundred niches in its sides which contain an equal number of images of Buddha. The walls present a series of historical or mythological episodes carved with minute detail in bas-reliefs like those at Nagkon Wat. Boro-Buddor is known to have been either a Buddhist or Jaina temple. It contains no inscription from which its age may be determined, though the traditional chronology of the Javanese ascribes its date to A. D. 1344. But it is a matter of certainty that the Hindoos were in Java during the thirteenth, fourteenth, and fifteenth centuries, and they doubtless built Boro-Buddor. Nagkon Wat was built, as I shall soon endeavor to show, about 1325, or nineteen years earlier than Boro-Buddor. Are we then to believe the Hindoos erected both of these Buddhist temples?

Perhaps the reader would ask me if there were no tablets eulogizing its founders or commemorating its establishment; no inscription concerning the building and the builders set up in Nagkon Wat. To which I should reply, Yes; inscriptions truly there are; some can be deciphered and others can not. But those which have been read only give descriptions of offerings made by different donors, with some allusions to religious ceremonies and mythological objects. There is a tablet of black marble, about five feet square, let into the wall of the eastern corridor, from which this information, and this alone, may be gained. The inscriptions which can not be read by the present race are written in ancient Cambodian, in characters that resemble the present alphabet, but have entirely dissimilar uses. It is said that several of the old kings introduced compulsory changes into the alphabet, besides altering the Cambodian era, and hence we see the almost hopeless confusion with which Orientalists have to contend in order to learn the chronology and history of this country. As further illustrative of these facts, the Pali—sister of the Sanskrit—is the sacred language of all the nations of Indo-China and Ceylon, though the mode of writing it in Ceylon is so unlike that practiced in Siam that the manuscripts of the one are not easily read by the priests of the other. What has been discovered of the Cambodian religious inscriptions would seem to indicate that they were derived or molded from the Pali or Sanskrit, rather than the Malay or Chinese languages. The hieroglyphics of Egypt have had a Champollion, the cuneiform inscriptions of Assyria have had a Rawlinson, the picture records of Central America have had an Aubin—now who will decipher for us the mysterious tablets of Angkor? Probably the feat will be achieved before long, though the difficulties are very great. It has been found that there are three styles of writing adopted, with characters fundamentally the same, which are modifications of the Devanagiri alphabet, or the ordinary form in which the Sanskrit is written; and that the Cambodians abbreviated the long Pali terms to suit their own monosyllabic speech, as do the Burmese to-day with their language, itself a variety of the ancient Pali. This they did on their momuments either by engraving the unpronounced part of a word or by carving the words as pronounced but not as written.

The Chinese traveler above mentioned, who wrote an account of his visit to Cambodia, notes the wonderful appearance of the capital, describes some of the manners of the people, among whom he noticed white women, but does not state whence they came. He says the king was covered with gold, pearls, and diamonds. Buddhism doubtless then prevailed in Cambodia, as he speaks of four-faced images of Buddha. From this writer's time until the latter part of the sixteenth century nothing authentic is heard. Cristoval de Jaque, a Portuguese, who, in 1570, being driven from Japan, took refuge in Cambodia, describes the ruins of this temple, and states that even then the inscriptions were unintelligible to the Cambodians, and that Angkor was no longer a royal residence, but had been deserted by its inhabitants. Cristoval says the Cambodians were the most potent people between the provinces of Burmah and Annam. Perhaps the name "Roma," so familiar to all Cambodians, was introduced by the Portuguese through the tenets of the Roman Catholic faith. But then why should their religion have become extinct and still the tradition of a Prince of Roma remain? In 1600 the Portuguese historian Ribodeneyra refers to Nagkon Wat as an ancient ruin. Then, again, there is a a long silence concerning these remains, which is not broken until the year 1860. Since this date the labors and studies of M. Mouhot and Dr. Bastian and Messrs. Kennedy and Thomson have brought the wonderful temples to the attention of the civilized world, and almost, as it were, discovered them for the first time.

And now, perhaps, I should state more definitely the results of my own study of the ruins. As to the race of people who built the city of Angkor, and the home of their descendants, I do not profess to have absolute knowledge. But as to when the temple of Nagkon Wat was built, I think I have satisfactorily determined, at least to within a few years. The mythology of Cambodia would take us back to a time coeval with the oldest monuments of Egypt. The more learned of the Cambodians give credence to neither of the traditions of 3,800 B. C. or of 525 B. C. as being the date of the founding of Angkor, but believe that it was founded A. D. 950, and was deserted in 1380, when the country was devastated by the Siamese. The late First King of Siam, who, it is known, had made considerable research into the past history of his country, said that the accounts of Farther India prior to A. D. 1250 were altogether unworthy of credit. Angkor, as I have said, was finally destroyed by the Siamese in 1380. Though the Chinese traveler (of 1295) gives a full account of all he saw there, he makes no mention of the great temple. Work upon Nagkon Wat was probably begun many years before 1380, because it seems to be the masterpiece of Cambodian art, and the empire was already in its decline in the middle of the fourteenth century. In an old Buddhist gateway in the Nankow Pass, about one hundred miles northeast of Pekin, in China, there are sculptures of the seven-headed snake, and also an inscription in Devanagiri characters, similar to those of Nagkon Wat, which bears the date 1345. Now, since we know the Cambodians sent embassies to China, it may fairly be inferred that this Chinese arch was built by Cambodian workmen. Hence I would conclude that the great temple was built somewhere between the dates just mentioned—say about 1325, or five hundred and sixty-five years ago. It would hardly be consistent with such meager evidence as we have to assign to Nagkon Wat a greater age than six hundred years, though possibly some of the ruins of Angkor city, and others in the surrounding provinces, may be a thousand or more years old. But this assignment of the origin of the great temple to so recent a date, in this instance, singularly enough, renders the problem of the present whereabouts of its builders all the more difficult of solution!

The old city of Uxmal, in Yucatan, almost rivals Angkor in extent, though it falls far short of it in the elegance and elaborate detail of its buildings. The climates of Yucatan and Cambodia are similar in their subjection to tropical rains, heat, summer dryness, and the very destructive powers of the vegetations by which they are covered. Stephens thought no monuments of Yucatan, retaining their forms, could be older than eight hundred years; and that none of those which are sufficiently perfect to be delineated, could be older than six hundred years. In other words, the majority of them belong to the great building epoch of the world—the fourteenth century. It seems very probable, therefore, that the origin of the great temple of Uxmal—the Casa de las Monjas—is contemporaneous with that of Angkor, the Nagkon Wat.

The principal ruins of Cambodia and Cochin-China yet discovered lie upon a plain about fifty miles in width in the province of Siamrap. The greater number of them are temples. Their design and execution show varying grades of art, which indicate varying periods of erection. The temple of Nagkon Wat, however, displays the most taste, and is the most beautiful and perfect of any of the remains. At about three miles from Angkor are the ruins of a city called Patentaphrohm, and near it is a temple about four hundred feet square, presenting the same combination of a royal and priestly residence as do Angkor and Nagkon Wat. Some of these temples and palaces, with their columns, sculptures, and statues, are nearly as interesting as those at Angkor. About four miles from Nagkon Wat are two other ancient remains—Bakong and Lailan. The former is a lofty pyramid, reared in the style of the Mexican teocalli. At the latter are several images of Buddha built of bricks which are exceedingly hard and made in a manner not understood now by the people of the country. They are polished and laid upon each other in so neat a manner that no traces of mortar can be discovered. In the province of Battambong, forty or fifty miles southwest of Siamrap town, there are also ruins of temples, monasteries and palaces; and, indeed, the whole valley of the Makong River, to the very borders of China, is spread with ruins of more or less magnitude, beauty, and interest.

Near the monastery of Prakeoh is an artificial lake built by the kings of Patentaphrohm, and surrounded with pleasure houses for their recreation. It must have been a work of immense labor, for the whole population of the Cambodia of to-day would scarcely be able to raise such a gigantic structure. The lake is of oblong shape, about half a mile broad and a mile long, and surrounded by a high embankment of solid masonry. Some of the blocks are as much as sixteen feet long and highly finished. In convenient places square platforms are built overhanging the water, with broad flights of steps leading down to it, and in such places the huge masses of stone laid on each other are embellished upon their ends by delicate chiseling, bearing the figures of serpents, eagles, and lions. In the middle of the lake is a small island with the remains of a former palace upon it.

The outer wall of Angkor city is now the only one at all preserved. It is about twenty feet in height and ten in width, built of large square blocks of coarse ferruginous stone, and has two gates upon the eastern side and one upon each of the others. A moat two hundred feet wide surrounds the city. The ancient city was two and a half miles in length and two and a quarter miles in width, surrounded by three walls, the outermost of which, the natives say, it would require an entire day to circumambulate. We entered by the south gateway—a pyramidal structure,

perhaps fifty feet in height, rising above a pointed arch.
On the top of this gateway was growing a poh tree, with
a trunk as much as three feet in diameter, which sent its
roots down through and over the huge blocks of stone
into the rich earth. The area within the walls is now
mostly overgrown with jungle. Excavations reveal nothing but rubbish of brick and pottery. About a mile north
from the gate is a colossal statue of Buddha, formed of
large stones, and evidently of modern fabrication. A
little farther on, in the midst of the forest, are the ruins
of an immense temple—some four hundred feet square—
a one-story building, inclosed by high walls and surmounted by fifty stone pagodas disposed in parallel rows.
These pagodas are about fifty feet in height, except the
central one, which was originally at least a hundred, and
upon their four sides are sculptured colossal faces of
Buddha, eight feet long by four feet in width. These
four-faced Buddhas wear a pleasant, good-natured expression, which is heightened by the corners of the mouth
curling upward. The ears are long and narrow, and slit
like those of the Burmese Gautama, but a rather fancy
tiara, or head-dress, takes the place of the short curls of
most Buddhas. These enormous heads recall the
Sphinxes of Egypt. One of them is nearly concealed by
a network of the roots of a tree which has grown up from
the side of the pagoda. To the poh trees and the ban-
yan and the fig are due in great part the present ruinous
state of this temple. These destroyers do their fell work
by insinuating their roots and branches into the walls.

Pagodas in the City of Angkor.

When we think of the climate, the ravages of war, the encroachments of the jungle, and the apathy of the present inhabitants, who do not repair them, we wonder at the present state of preservation of many of the ruins. Still it is doubtful if these grand monuments can defy time much longer. Some of the blocks of stone in the pagodas are separated by as much as an inch, and many seem only to require a touch to tumble them to the ground. I saw a solid block of stone, six feet in length, which was supported in a nearly horizontal position solely by the roots of an immense poh tree. Some chambers of this temple are entirely choked up, and over and through all the ruins the parasitical poh has spread its roots and reared aloft its glossy green head, while shrubs and coarse grass now riot where once the praises of the great Buddha —the Illuminator of the World—resounded through the halls. Thus eternal nature effaces evanescent art; thus monument and hieroglyphic are concealed beneath the envious arabesque of leaf and flower.

About half a mile from here we came to the palace gate of the inner, or third wall, upon one side of which, on an immense stone platform, rests the statue of the Leper King—of him who is supposed to have founded or at least completed the building of Angkor. The sides of the platform are faced with slabs of stone, covered with different featured and costumed figures, all sitting in cross-legged positions. On the opposite side of the gateway are pictures in stone—a battle and a military procession. What remains of the palace is a structure of pyramidal form, terminating in a tower, the whole probably one hundred and fifty feet in height. It is much dilapidated. From the staircase the sandstone has fallen away, and the underlying coarse volcanic rock is much worn. In a small room near the summit were long inscriptions engraved upon the jambs of the doors, in the ancient undecipherable Cambodian characters.

The statue of the Leper King is carved from sandstone in a sitting posture. The body, although naked and rather rudely cut, yet exhibits a marked contrast to the physical type of the present race of Cambodians. The features are of a much higher order; indeed, the profile is quite Grecian in outline. The eyes are closed; a thin mustache, twisted up at the ends, covers the upper lip; the ears are long, and have the immense holes in their lobes peculiar to the Burmese and Siamese images of Buddha; the hair is thick and displayed in curls upon the head, the top of which is surmounted by a small round crown. It is said that men having features like the statue of the leprous king may be occasionally met with at the present day in the mountains of Annam. There is an inscription in ancient Cambodian characters upon the front of the pedestal. The natives, with astonishing forethought, have placed a small grass thatch over this statue. They have also somewhat naturalized (if a foreigner) and very much travestied their royal ancestor (if indeed such he be) by blackening his teeth, rouging his lips, and gilding his forehead. Of course the precise history of the Leper King is not known. One tradition affirms that Angkor was founded in fulfillment of a vow by a king who was a leper.   Another tradition says that to an Egyptian king who, for some sacrilegious deed was turned into a leper, must be ascribed the authorship of Angkor.

We returned to our camp, took a parting look at Nagkon Wat, and then started for Siamrap.   Here my companions took leave of me and set out on their return to Bangkok, while I continued on alone to Saigon, crossing first Thalaysap, the great sweet-water lake of Cambodia, next descending the Mesap River to Panompin, the capital, and then on again till finally the metropolis of Cochin-China was safely and happily reached.   I had thus traversed the great Indo-Chinese peninsula—riding over its plains and through its forests, voyaging across its lakes, and paddling down its rivers—a distance of nearly seven hundred miles in six weeks, including many long and delightful delays by the way.   And I had assured myself that a richer field for Oriental research nowhere exists than in Cambodia.

III.

QUARANTINED IN THE ANTILLES.

FOR some days I had been waiting at La Guayra, the principal seaport of Venezuela, for a steamer going to Trinidad, whence I hoped to be able to get to Barbadoes; but as the small-pox was then raging at Aspinwall, from which the eastward bound steamer sailed, there was a strong probability of my being quarantined in Trinidad and elsewhere. It was necessary, however, to "take the chances." The steamer which I selected was the Colombie, a fine large vessel of three thousand tons belonging to the Compagnie Générale Transatlantique. We had about twenty first-class passengers, and a cargo of coffee, cacao, cotton, and sugar. As we steamed rapidly out of the harbor and turned to the eastward, the coast presented a series of rough ranges of mountains, those nearest the sea being red and brownish and covered with cacti, a second and higher range behind showing some good grazing land, and some still further back being covered with trees. Near La Guayra were large sugar-cane plantations and factories. But going on, the land appeared very sterile and uninhabited. During the night we passed the towns of New Barcelona and Cumana, the latter being famous as the spot where Humboldt first landed in the New World, and where he resided for a long time, engaged in astronomical and meteorological researches. Morning showed upon our left the large island of Margarita, belonging to Venezuela and settled mostly by fishermen. About noon we ran in to the roadstead of Carupano, on the mainland, and a little village of single-story houses lining the shore of a small semicircular bay. It was backed by hills, some of which were cultivated and others covered with scrubby vegetation and trees. This place is the outlet of a very rich coffee and cacao region, and hence all the great lines of steamers make it a point of call. We loaded much coffee, and then went on to the British island of Trinidad, whose capital, the Port-of-Spain, has a very good circular roadstead. The town, however, lies upon such level ground and is so thickly set with trees that but little of it appears from the steamer's deck. Beyond are beautiful green hills, many of them planted with sugar-cane. As I feared, the steamer was quarantined, and no passengers were allowed to land. So I went on to Fort de France, in the island of Martinique, the next port, hoping to be allowed to land there, and so get to Barbadoes. At Port-of-Spain we loaded a great deal of coffee. On leaving, our course was nearly due north. We sighted the British island of Grenada and also the archipelago of small islands extending from Grenada to St. Vincent and called the Grenadines.

At eight o'clock the following morning we were in plain sight of Martinique, styled the most beautiful of the Lesser Antilles. It is about fifty miles in length and fifteen miles at its greatest breadth. It has a population of about one hundred and fifty thousand, of whom only twenty thousand are whites. The shape and surface of the island are very irregular, and the coast is broken up into numerous bays, which are difficult of entry. The formation is decidedly volcanic, and the conical hills, one of which, Mont Pelée, reaches a height of forty-five hundred feet, are all extinct volcanoes. The surface is greatly diversified with fertile valleys, watered by small rivers. The higher parts of the hills are thickly timbered, while the undulating plains are covered with sugar-cane or great velvety meadows. The varieties of yellow and green color seen under a bright morning sun were very pretty. The principal productions of the island are sugar, coffee, indigo, maize, and cocoa. The commerce is chiefly with France. There are two towns, Fort de France and St. Pierre, of which the former, being the seat of government, is considered the capital, although St. Pierre far exceeds it in size and commercial importance. Fort de France is a neat little town situated in a small valley opening directly upon the ocean, or rather upon the northern side of a very large bay which here reaches into the island from the ocean. The roadstead is circular, and is so surrounded by land as to be very safe for shipping. Just before the town at one side is an enormous fort, built in two terraces with great stone walls and towers. The houses of Fort de

France are two stories in height, and the foliage about
them, consisting of cocoanut trees and acacias and others
in full flower, makes a very picturesque scene.   Little
steamers ply from here to St. Pierre and to other points
where either settlements or produce would warrant
transport service.   We were quarantined at Fort de
France as well as at Port-of-Spain.   Such passengers
as left the steamer would have to remain in quarantine
for four days, and should any of them die during that
time the detention of the survivors in the lazaretto
would be greatly extended.   So I decided to go on to
the town of Basse Terre in the island of Guadeloupe,
there to endeavor to catch the Royal Mail steamer to
Barbadoes.   We were busy during the remainder of the
day taking coal from lighters, which were manned by
negroes of large stature and splendid physical development.   The negroes of these French islands are not only
fine looking, but remarkably intelligent.   Many small
boats also came off to us from the shore, whose occupants
had for sale choice shells and corals, collections of prepared fishes, and curious radiates which were dried and
varnished.   Some of the fish were covered with long
spines like a porcupine, and many others were equally odd
to northern eyes.   The women had besides for sale various kinds of potted fruits, and pin-cushions fringed with
pretty bead trimmings.

The next afternoon we started for St. Pierre.   The
scenery continued interesting—hills, plantations, woods,
valleys, rocky coasts, and little houses half concealed by

13

the rich foliage. It was quite dark when we reached St. Pierre, though with the assistance of a small moon, my binoculars, and the lights of the city, I could make out something of its position and general appearance. It extends along the coast and up a broad and very gently sloping valley, and is backed by high and prettily diversified hills. We were quarantined and not allowed to land, for which, however, there would not have been time, as we remained but about an hour, and then started for Basse Terre, on the island of Guadeloupe, passing the British island of Dominica, of which more anon. We found Basse Terre to be a small town built along the coast and sloping back to the base of some high and steep hills. We remained less than an hour—no passengers being allowed to land—and then, turning about and rounding the southern end of the island, headed north for Point à Pitre. Guadeloupe consists properly of two islands separated by a narrow channel which is only five miles in length but is navigable for small vessels. The western island, or Basse Terre (Guadeloupe proper), is thirty-five miles long and eighteen miles wide; the eastern is a little smaller. The larger island is traversed by a mountain range, the highest point of which is a volcano, called La Souffrière, whose summit is five thousand feet above the level of the sea. Like Martinique, Guadeloupe is of volcanic origin; it is, like the other, subject to destructive earthquakes and hurricanes. The exports are the same, with the addition of rum, tobacco, and dyewoods from Guadeloupe. The eastern part of Guadeloupe proper presents some of the most beautiful scenery in the Antilles. From the summit of La Souffrière, as we passed, a thin column of smoke curled upward. The surface slopes gently back from the ocean to the central range of hills, and is covered mostly with sugar-cane. Several streams descend from springs in the hills. A few villages appear. Grande Terre seems to be low-lying, flat, and swampy. The town of Point à Pitre stands on this island, at the mouth of the channel or river above spoken of, and was formerly the capital, but is now an uninteresting place, though with a fine harbor. The next stopping-place of my steamer being Santander, in Spain, it became imperative that I should disembark at Point à Pitre, notwithstanding an unavoidable quarantine, which I soon learned would be eight days in length. There were seven first-class and thirty third-class passengers who were to be quarantined with me; so, if misery loves company, I was well provided for. The seven—among whom were two ladies—were all of different nationalities; the thirty, men and women, were either French or English negroes. In a few hours we were transferred to a small sloop, together with our baggage and some provisions. The steamer left us, for Europe, and we hoisted sail for the quarantine station, situated upon one of the little group called Les Saintes, which lie south of Guadeloupe and about thirty miles from Point à Pitre. Several other neighboring islands besides Les Saintes are included within the jurisdiction of Guadeloupe. Our sloop was a miserable, dirty, old, worn-out craft, and first and third

class passengers were huddled together in the most social-
istic manner. We sailed along the beautiful eastern shore
of Guadeloupe, slowly at first, as we had a head wind;
and then the wind gave out altogether, and we were becalmed for several hours. The negro passengers amused
themselves by continual brawls and fights among themselves, and the crew by drinking rum, which soon made
most of them drunk. A breeze sprang up in the evening,
and we finally reached our destination and dropped anchor near shore. It was midnight and too late to sum-
mon the medical inspector from the neighboring town.
Without his official survey and examination we could not
land, so we had to sit in the boat—there was not room to
lie down—until morning.

Not until eight o'clock the next day did the doctor
present himself and give us the necessary permission to
land. At a little stone pier the manager of the quarantine
station checked off our names, and learned which of the
three classes of accommodation we wished, the charges
being for the first class seven francs per day, three francs
for the second, and one franc for the third. We were
allowed to take only our satchels with us. Many events
of the next few days were of a very farcical character.
The first absurdity presented to us was a man who, with
a big brush dipped in a large basin of carbolic acid,
sprinkled a few drops upon the back of each of us. The
"Lazarat des Saintes," as the quarantine station of Guadeloupe is officially styled, is very prettily situated upon a
narrow neck of land over which strong ocean trade winds

continually sweep. The buildings are placed at the bottom and upon the side of a circular hill surmounted by an old battery, which is about five hundred feet above sea-level. This hill terminates the island in this direction, and from its top splendid views may be had of Guadeloupe to the north, Marie Galante to the east, Dominica to the south, and the several islands of Les Saintes around and below. The islands of Les Saintes, like all the rest, are of volcanic formation, hilly, rocky, covered with coarse grass and scrubby trees. They produce coffee and cotton by cultivation; some sugar-cane is also grown. All the islands are sparsely inhabited. The people depend largely upon sheep and fish for their sustenance. They are mostly negroes and creoles, who speak a very bad sort of French. The water where our sloop anchored was very deep and clear and full of enormous fish, which we could plainly see at a depth of fifty feet. Along the shore are beds of beautiful corals and many varieties of shells. There are accommodations in the quarantine for about five hundred people. The buildings are long, narrow, single story, built of wood, with shingled sides and roof. Those of the first class have a broad hall extending throughout their entire length, on each side of which are small rooms whose partitions reach only to the eaves. At one end is a large dining and sitting room. The buildings of the other classes are all open, like the wards of a hospital. Our rooms were exceedingly plain, being furnished with little more than small iron bedsteads. The table was fairly good, and we readily learned to what

we were entitled from a printed set of rules which was
posted in the dining-room. We were furnished with just
such things, at just such meals, and in just such quan-
tities—grammes and centigrammes, litres and centilitres.
The printed rules not only specify exactly the kind and
amount of our food, but also the number of mattresses,
pillows, sheets, towels, and napkins we are to be allowed.
They mention the rather extraordinary fact that bed
linen and towels are to be washed only every fifteen days,
while the table linen and napkins are washed as frequently
as every eight days. A doctor arrived from Basse Terre
the morning following our advent, and remained with
us during the continuance of our quarantine. He had a
little detached house all to himself, and made use of a
small pharmacy established in a room of our dormitory.
Soon after the arrival of the doctor our trunks were
brought on shore and placed in a large stone building
near the wharf. Here they were opened, and all soiled
linen was required to be removed and hung upon lines.
Small basins of sulphur were distributed about, and, being
ignited, the building was closed and our effects thus fumi-
gated for forty-eight hours. The door was then opened,
the soiled linen removed and dipped into boiling salt
water, and all the pillows used by the passengers were
piled in a heap upon the shore and burned by the doctor.
It was then permitted us to have our trunks sent to our
rooms. Of course, all this was very inconsistent and of
very little value as a prophylactic measure, for most of
us had soiled linen in our satchels, at our rooms, and

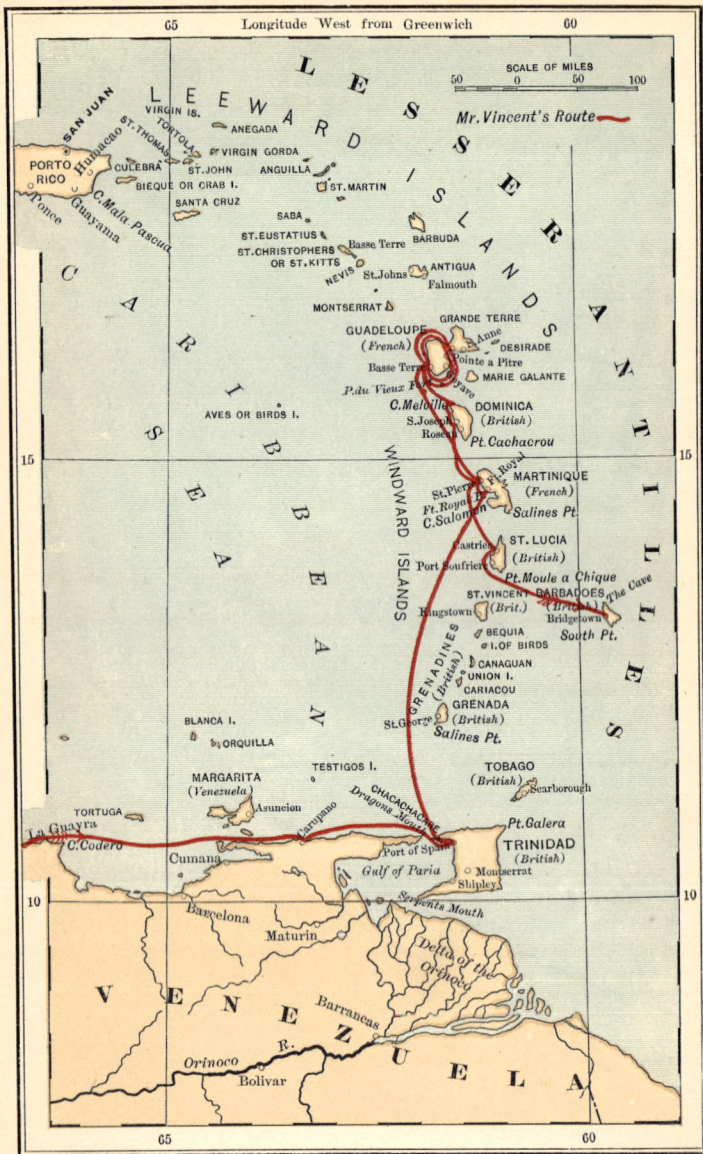

The Lesser Antilles, West Indies, with Route of the Author.

nothing was done about fumigating this. The same day
that this red-tape tomfoolery was consummated we were
all required to pay in advance for the proposed term of
our detention in quarantine. Anything not furnished
our table which we desired—such as liquors, preserves,
or pickles—we had to obtain in the neighboring town,
through means of our daily market boat. For such additions we had, of course, to pay from our own pockets.
We found it quite comfortable in quarantine while remaining in the breeze. We were allowed to take a swim
in the bay every morning. Occasionally we would go
out fishing, and this, with walks, reading, writing, and
card-playing, caused our time to pass very quickly.

On the morning of the ninth day we leave the quarantine of Les Saintes for Basse Terre, a sail of a couple
of hours. We land at a pier and then walk across a small
plaza—filled with tamarind trees and containing an iron
fountain in its center—to the custom-house. Opposite
this, in the single hotel of the place, we obtain fair accommodation. The town is laid out at right angles, and
those streets which lead up toward the hills are paved with
square stone blocks, as are also the sidewalks, the other
streets being macadamized. There is running water in
most of the streets, and the town is besides well supplied
with water from a small river which courses through it.
At the corners of the streets kerosene lamps are suspended. The principal business street contains small
retail stores of every kind. Back upon the hills are the
dwellings of the richer merchants, imbedded in lovely

flower gardens. The market of Basse Terre is held in an open square filled with beautiful acacias. Here you will be sure to discover a fine variety of fruits and plenty of fish; other departments of the vegetable kingdom are less worthily represented. The cathedral is a plain stone structure, with only a few plaster statues outwardly, but within it is very pretty. The ceilings contain portraits of the evangelists, the walls plaster casts of the " stations of Christ." There are several large paintings and a fine organ. About the only other show sight of Basse Terre is its Jardin des Plantes, which is small, but contains a splendid collection of rare tropical plants tastefully arranged with lawns, ponds, fountains, walks, summer-houses, etc. An interesting drive of seven miles takes the stranger directly back into the island to the military barracks and a small village situated upon the flanks of the volcano of La Souffrière. A handsome large hospital commands superb views of ocean, town, and island. Good macadamized roads are found all over Guadeloupe. A diligence runs each day to Point à Pitre, about forty-five miles distant, and a little steamer also connects these places three times in every week. You rarely see a white face in Guadeloupe save that of one of the garrison, but there is every shade from this to the blackest of coal. The common people are simply and thinly clad, as is necessary in so torrid a spot. The men wear linen shirt and trousers and go barefooted; the women gay-colored calico dresses, the waists of which come up just under the arms. No corsets or stockings are worn. Upon their heads they wear yellow silk bandannas, and a red kerchief around the neck. The upper classes imitate French fashions for the most part. Very many of the ladies dress in black, which becomes them amazingly. But it is always amusing to see an otherwise completely and properly dressed lady with bare feet thrust into French high-heeled patent-leather shoes or slippers.

One day I made an excursion in the little iron steamer to Point à Pitre. The route is up the west coast, and around the northern, to the little salt river that divides the two islands which together constitute Guadeloupe. We left at eight in the morning and arrived at three in the afternoon, making half a dozen stops at little villages on the way. We kept within a short distance of the shore, and hence enjoyed splendid views all day long. The island presented the same general characteristics as those already described — beautiful hills covered with trees or coffee and fertile valleys filled with sugar-cane or maize. Here and there might be seen a farm-house and sugar-factory. Numbers of the graceful cabbage-palm inland, and cocoanut-palms and bananas nearer the shore, lent a foreign and tropical aspect to the scene. We had already passed upon the left the British island of Montserrat, and as we turned in toward Grande Terre, we could just discern the dim outline of another English island to the north—Antigua. The salt-water channel is never more than fifty feet wide, and is lined with mangroves. We found a number of ships lying off Point à Pitre, as upon a former visit, and upon landing discovered a town of similar character to Basse Terre. The streets, however, are generally wider, and the houses two and three stories in height. The cathedral is a fine large building with stained-glass windows, a marble altar, and many paintings. I returned the next day by the same steamer to Basse Terre. Breakfast was served on board and was very bad, notwithstanding five francs were charged for it. As regards the steamer, it was, perhaps, with a single exception—an Egyptian one in the Mediterranean—the most filthy vessel it was ever my misfortune to encounter. I remained about a week in Basse Terre, trying to get a steamer to take me on my way, but, owing to a report of yellow fever at Point à Pitre, the whole island of Guadeloupe was declared in quarantine. Although several steamers called—among them the large French steamer Amérique, of five thousand tons burden, which used to ply between New York and Havre—they did not "communicate" with the shore, and passengers were not received. Finally, seeing no chance of leaving Basse Terre for some weeks, a few of us who had been at Les Saintes together decided to sail in a small boat to the next large island to the south, Dominica, a British island with which we heard the Royal Mail steamers communicated, and from which we might get to Barbadoes.

We left at four o'clock one morning, our destination being a small port on the northern end of Dominica, where we proposed to transship to a boat of that island, and go on to Roseau, its capital. Roseau is, by this course, about fifty miles from Basse Terre. Our boat was exceedingly small for the number of our party and the weight of our baggage. It was quite open, about fifteen feet in length and four feet in width, and was sloop-rigged. The passengers were four, the crew three. No other boat was to be had in Basse Terre, and so we felt bound to make a dash for liberty at almost any risk. It was rather a dangerous journey, as we were loaded to within a few inches of the gunwale, and the sea—the open ocean—between the islands of Guadeloupe and Dominica is generally rough. It would, moreover, owing to the amount of our baggage have been extremely difficult to bale our boat should very heavy rains visit us or violent squalls force water aboard. Fortunately, we had no rain and no strong winds. We were on the contrary gently wafted by light breezes or becalmed so that we had to row. The sun beat upon us with such terrific force that we became almost sick. Fortunately, we had taken a good supply of provisions and drinking water. We sailed and rowed and drifted for eighteen hours, crowded in the boat so that we could not change our positions an atom. We reached our destination at ten in the evening and slept on the floor of a native's hut until four the next morning, when we engaged a large four-oared boat and men to row us to a neighboring village, where we hoped to get from the harbor-master a permit which we could take to Roseau with us. Imagine our surprise and disgust when this official said he could do nothing for us, but would be compelled to put us in quarantine for at least a couple of days, while he forwarded our explanation and petition to the President of Dominica, at Roseau!

The town of Prince Rupert where we had called—we were not allowed to go on shore—is most picturesquely situated upon level ground, at the head of a deep circular bay, with rows of beautiful cocoanut-palms along the shore and beautiful hills as a background. The quarantine station is situated on the side of a tree-covered hill, on the north headland of the bay. Here there is an old and very large stone fortress, at present ruined and dismantled and overgrown with trees and shrubs. It appears that it was the intention of the Government first to make Prince Rupert the capital, but the unhealthfulness of the position being discovered, the idea was abandoned. The enormously thick stone walls of the fort are, however, still standing, as well as part of those of the barracks, mess-halls, kitchens, hospital, and lock-up. The various outlying batteries and the fortress and its equipment, erected about a century ago, are said to have cost one million dollars. A narrow stone causeway leads from the landing up the hill to the fortress. Passing through a great guava orchard, we entered the massive gateway, and were surprised and shocked to find that the only quarantine accommodation for all classes consisted of an old stone kitchen, about fifteen feet by nine, with a miserable leaky roof and broken floor, full of venomous insects and disgusting vermin, and filthy beyond expression. It contained not a single article of furniture and no toilet conveniences of any character. These things, as well as the table crockery, we were obliged to hire from the harbor-master. This official also agreed to furnish us with meals, which were dispatched from Prince Rupert, across the bay, a distance of a couple of miles, and thus arrived in a lukewarm or cold condition. For all these things we were expected, of course, to pay liberally. Our first act, upon making the above interesting discoveries, was to send a petition to the President of Dominica, begging him to have our quarantine made very brief, or omitted altogether, in view of the frightful condition of our quarters, which were so unsanitary, and in such a hot and airless situation, that we feared we could not remain without serious, if not fatal illness. We intimated, in brief, that the old kitchen was not fit for human habitation, and in this view were supported by both the health officer and the officer in charge of the quarantine. The latter informed us that a few years ago suitable accommodation existed in the neighboring barracks, but that a hurricane removed its roof, and another had never been added. During the afternoon a smart shower came up, and we found that our roof leaked in sixteen places. We had to pile all our baggage in one corner, and move our chairs as the descending douches consecutively occurred. At night we were so pestered with vermin—mosquitoes, fleas, ants, spiders, mice—that sleep was quite impossible. Examining our quarters more carefully early in the morning, we readily enumerated twenty distinct species of venomous insects, and of these there were many varieties.

On the third day the health officer arrived with an
order from the Board of Health at Roseau commuting
our quarantine from fifteen days, the advertised period, to
three. So the following morning, early, we left for Roseau in the same four-oared boat that had brought us
to the quarantine station. We kept near the shore in
smooth water. The island consisted of lofty and irregular wooded hills, beautiful valleys with steep sides, and a
little level land occasionally near the shore. Many very
small rivers entered the sea; indeed, there are said to be
nearly four hundred of these little streams in Dominica.
Little cultivation of the land was visible, owing to its
very rough and broken character. We passed a number
of villages like those in Central Africa, their huts oblong
in shape, with steep grass-thatched roofs, and single opening—the door. These villages were generally situated at
the mouth of some stream, and were half-concealed by
the ever-picturesque cocoanut-palms. The surf thun-
dered upon the beach in very majestic style, rolling the
pebbles up and down with sonorous boomings. After six
hours of sailing and rowing, we reached Roseau, a little
town at the opening of a beautiful valley sloping up from
the sea, on which it presents but a narrow front. Away
back, upon a high cliff with a perpendicular face, stands
an old fort, now utilized as a hospital. Three or four
schooners were anchored abreast of the town as we disem-
barked at the solitary pier and then walked a short distance up one of the roughly paved, surface-drained, grass-
grown streets to the sole hotel. This we were delighted

to find clean and comfortable, and offering a good table. The little houses of Roseau are generally of wood, with shingle roofs, and but one story in height. They are not generally painted, either within or without. Thus exteriorly the town presents a very somber grayish appearance. The cathedral is of cut gray stone, is low but large, and contains a pulpit of dark polished wood, which was presented by the late Emperor Napoleon III. This unfortunate monarch had, I believe, some distant relatives living here.

One day a party from our hotel made an excursion up the valley to visit a lime plantation and a beautiful waterfall in the Roseau River, about ten miles distant from the capital. We were all mounted upon tough ponies, and carried rubber coats as a protection from the heavy and frequently occurring showers. The road for the first part of the way was very good, wide enough and level enough for a carriage. We passed the river on a neat iron-girder bridge, and soon entered a part of the valley like a gorge, or cañon, with steep and lofty walls. The scenery became most wild and picturesque. The density of the vegetation was especially remarkable; every square inch of surface seemed packed with verdure. Even the rocky precipices were covered with trees, scrub, and vines. Prominent features were the cocoanut-palms, bananas, bamboos, breadfruit, almond trees, papaya, mangoes, tree ferns, and plantations of sugar-cane, limes, and cacao. Dominica possesses in a remarkable degree the two requisites for rank vegetation — intense heat and frequent showers. The road gradually ascended to a height of perhaps fifteen hundred feet, when we reached the lime plantation to which we were bound. There were some two hundred acres under cultivation. The trees were so heavily covered with the beautiful golden fruit that nearly all of them had to have their limbs supported by pieces of bamboo. The limes were being crushed in a small mill worked by a yoke of oxen. The juice ran into large hogsheads from which it was taken to have oil distilled from it. Afterward a process of boiling condensed it to one sixth of its original quantity, when it was bottled and shipped as the concentrated oil of commerce. Near by, the owner of the plantation had a very comfortable little house, surrounded by beautiful trees, lawns, and flowers. After inspecting the premises and breakfasting, we rode on up the valley, the trail becoming very steep and frequently zigzagging. Superb views were obtained of the valley below us, of lateral gorges, and of mountain peaks upon every hand. We next entered a dense forest, and continued in it until we reached the neighborhood of the fall, where we had to alight and proceed on foot. The fall, though narrow, contains considerable water, and makes a nearly perpendicular leap of two hundred feet. We returned by the same road to the farm-house where we had breakfasted, and in the cool of the late afternoon remounted our ponies and went back to town after a most agreeable excursion, notwithstanding that the trip from the falls to the farm-house was made through a tremendous rainstorm such as can be experienced only in the tropics. Dominica was formerly devoted to the raising of sugar-cane, but now it can not compete with some of the other islands; and, besides, the sugar markets of the world are overstocked, so that ground formerly covered with cane is now occupied by limes. These are hardy trees, and require little or no cultivation, while the cane requires a great deal.

Dominica produces comparatively little of anything, it has so small a proportion of level ground; but, if behind in the matter of cultivation, it is certainly well to the front as regards picturesqueness. Martinique has, as I have already said, long been styled the most beautiful of the Lesser Antilles, but Dominica will well contest with her the palm.

A few days afterward we left Roseau in one of the Royal Mail steamships for Barbadoes. This steamer had called at Basse Terre, but had not communicated with the shore; so, after all, it was most fortunate that we went from Guadeloupe to Dominica. We called at St. Pierre, in Martinique, and then at Port Castries, in the British island of St. Lucia, and the next stop was at Barbadoes—that Barbadoes for which I had set out from La Guayra just five weeks before!

IV.

AN ORIENTAL MONSTER.

SOME ten years ago, the startling and atrocious news came from Burmah that young King Theebau, seeking to appease the wrath of the evil spirits in which he was said to believe, had buried alive seven hundred men, women, and children. The report was contradicted, and may have been, in great part, untrue; but, nevertheless, the "institutions" which afflicted Burmah gave color to almost any amount of credulity vouchsafed by the reader of the daily journals.

For instance, the Government of Burmah was a pure despotism. It therefore protected the chief ruler in any crime, however horrible or nefarious, he may have chosen to perpetrate, and enabled him, with impunity, to hold the lives and fortunes of his subjects in the hollow of his hand. He was the father of the state; the mandarins and the magistrates bore a similar relation to the provinces and departments over which they respectively presided. The laws were created in accordance with the grossest instincts of savagery, and were the full expression of ferocious principles, of which certain laws in our own country may be regarded as faint reverberations. Bribery thrived in the rankest luxuriance. What was there named justice was founded upon the celebrated Institutes of Menu; but the most unfortunate thing that could happen to a citizen was to fall into its clutches, unless he was rich enough to buy himself out. If a litigant was wealthy, the suit was apt to be a long and costly one, and a decision was frequently given in favor of him who paid the highest. A favorite mode of trial was that by ordeal. In accordance with this principle of equity, the party that could remain the longer beneath the surface of the water, or that showed the more endurance in immersing his finger in boiling water or melted lead, was in the right, and came forth victor. Punishments were extremely cruel. For murder and treason, decapitation, drowning, and burning alive were most in vogue. For offenses less heinous, maiming, branding, imprisonment, slavery, the stocks, and laboring in chains were held in reserve. Cruel floggings were all but universal, and were inflicted even upon the highest officers of the state. There, as in China, the bamboo was the invariable instrument; and the fear of the cane, which, in these regions, is the beginning of wisdom, may be said to have influenced all eastern Asia. The system of forfeits and fines was more rigorous than that prescribed by Mosaic law. If a man stole a horse, he must surrender two; if an ox, he must surrender fifteen; a buffalo, thirty; a pig, fifty; a young fowl, one hundred; a man, ten—or four if he only concealed him. These requirements, indeed, were the best part of Burmese law. The fact which I wish to emphasize is that, in the main, the laws were cruel and justice meant injustice.

The kingdom of which I am speaking is a very secluded portion of Farther India, and is now, as is well known, under an English protectorate. The locality is between Hindoostan and the Bay of Bengal on the west, and Siam on the east. Mandalay, the capital, is on the great Irrawaddy River, about seven hundred miles from its mouth. The city is nearly a mile square, and is surrounded by a high brick wall. Macadamized avenues, one hundred feet wide, intersect each other at right angles. The grass-roofed houses, mostly built of bamboo, are raised a few feet from the ground on posts; in some of the principal streets, however, the structures are of wood, and are two stories in height. Lying upon a plain, the general aspect would be very monotonous but for the pagodas, monasteries, and image-houses which sprout up in every direction and lend diversity of contour and color. The population may be placed at one hundred thousand. The trade is mainly controlled by Chinese merchants. At the time of my visit, a number of years ago, less than a score of European residents were there. These were mostly officials of the British Government, which, since the previous war, had always maintained a political agent at the capital. Upon the advent of the present King, that officer became convinced that wisdom demanded his withdrawal. The entire population of Burmah is not more than thirty-five hundred thousand;

the whole extent of territory is six hundred miles in length and four hundred in width.

The King, who once alone decided upon peace or war, and who dispensed at pleasure imprisonment, torture, and death, resides in a palace, the surrounding walls of which are double, the inner walls inclosing seventy-five acres of ground. Within this space are found the royal pagodas, temples, barracks, mint, law courts, monasteries, military store-houses, and, finally, the magnificent Hall of Audience, built of dark wood intricately carved and gayly ornamented. Here is the abode of the white elephant; here are the library and the various palaces of the King and royal family; and it is needless to say that the families of the pre-eminently married potentates of Asia necessitate a perfect labyrinth of imperial residences. The style of architecture in all these fabrics is highly ornate. The roofs are lofty and pyramidal, and the edifices are always built upon piles raised five or six feet from the ground. The King, dwelling here in the midst of his wives and favorites, had the satisfaction of knowing that the entire domain of Burmah was owned by the Crown. His revenue was five million dollars; but this sum proving too trifling for his orgies, he created lotteries, to which his subjects were forced to subscribe. This method of raising money was quite as effective as that of the former King, which was to buy goods at a very cheap rate, and to serve them out at a very dear one as pay to his troops and followers. These grossly badgered victims were afterward forced to sell the goods at an enormous sacrifice.

It was in this barbarously magnificent residence that King Theebau had the hourly opportunity of snuffing up that incense of flattery of which most monarchs, whether civilized or uncivilized, can scarcely have too much. He was not only " Lord of Life and Death," but enjoyed a score of other titles. Among these were : Mighty Lord ; Glorious Sovereign of Land and Sea ; Possessor of Mines of Rubies, Amber, Gold, Silver, and all Kinds of Metals ; the Lord under whose Command were Innumerable Soldiers, Captains, and Generals ; the Lord who was King of many Countries and Provinces, and Emperor over many Rulers and Princes who waited round the Throne with the Badges of his Authority ; the Lord who was adorned with the Greatest Power, Wisdom, Knowledge, Prudence, and Forethought ; the Lord who was rich in the Possession of Elephants and Horses, and, in particular, was the Lord of Many White Elephants ; the Lord who was the Greatest of Kings, the Most Just, and the Most Religious, the Master of Life and Death ; Sovereign of all the Umbrella-bearing Chiefs ; the Sun-descended Monarch. In announcing these appellations categorically, the royal chamberlain needed a cultivated memory ; but probably his recollection of past bamboos and his dread of future ones, produced as fine an effect as the best system of *memoria technica.*

When I first saw the gentleman who enjoyed these titles he was occupying a position which, though neither comfortable nor dignified, was in accordance with the strictest etiquette of the Burmese court. I was at that

time honored with an audience with his father—an event
which I have described at some length in The Land of
the White Elephant. The crown-prince was a tall, slight
young man, with fine piercing eyes and an unusually
intelligent expression. The simplicity of his attire was
slightly contradicted by the presence of two enormous
diamond ear-rings. This simplicity he retained after
ascending the throne, when the ornaments which principally distinguished his appearance from that of an ordinary Burmese citizen were a spray of diamonds worn
in his hair, and worth the value of a province, and a
ring whose solitary sapphire was doubtless the richest
in the world. His extreme handsomeness rendered his
attitude on the above - mentioned occasion the more
noticeable. He was lying at full length, face downward,
before the throne, his nose literally touching the floor.
Upon the royal dais sat his august father, King Mounglon, in shirtless majesty. Mounglon died in 1878, and
the Executive Council, consisting of the four principal
ministers of state, immediately elected Theebau to the
throne. Absolute authority proved more than the un-
trained mind of the young man could bear. Instead of
seeking advice from his father's old and trusted councilors,
ors, he surrounded himself with young men and min-
ions of his own age, and began that career of debauchery
in which he proved so signal a success. He emulated
those ancient heroes of infamy who are known to history
as the rulers of Rome, and probably no crime accomplished by them has been left unachieved by him. In

this manner he became known to the world. He disposed of claimants to the throne by immediately putting to death all who in the remotest degree could feel an interest in that direction. The doings of Herod, Nero, and the King of Dahomey pale their ineffectual fires and hide their diminished heads compared with those of this Eastern majesty. Of the hundred and ten children left by his royal father, all but three were put to the slaughter. One could not call the King of Burmah "brother" without feeling that the executioner was on his track. Some of these princes and princesses were flogged to death, others were buried alive, many were drawn and quartered, and not a few were blown to atoms with gunpowder.

Several ancestors of Theebau have, I believe, acted quite as badly. The dynasty extends back for one hundred and thirty years, and is stained with bloody crimes. One of the old kings drowned his uncle, who was said to have conspired against him, and then proceeded to pass his life in fishing and drinking. His fondness for water was confined to that in which he found his piscatory pleasures, and he soon procured for himself the name of the "drunken fishing king." Another ancestor, no further back than 1781, reigned only seven days. He was then deposed, placed in a red sack, and thrown into the river, his queens and concubines being burned alive. His successor destroyed an entire village where a conspiracy had been discovered. All the inhabitants, young and old, and of both sexes, were dragged forth and committed to the flames. Even the priests did not escape. All perished together on a gigantic pile of wood which had been erected for that infernal purpose. The village houses were then razed, the ground was plowed, and a stone was erected as a commemoration, a malediction, and a warning. One king used to punish his delinquent ministers by spreading them upon their backs in the glare of the sun, with weights on their chests, till they expired. From 1837 to 1845 King Tharawadi led a life of the most royal debauchery and imperial intoxication. His favorite pastime was to assassinate a once favorite minister or companion who had suddenly become inimical. He paid the penalty of this murderous sport by being smothered to death in the recesses of his palace. His amiable son and successor devoted his regal genius to cock-fighting, ram-fighting, and gambling. To compile a catalogue of the executions that took place during his reign would tire the wrist and patience of a Hercules. King Theebau, therefore, may be thought worthy of the blood which sends its ferocious corpuscles coursing through his veins.

The people of Burmah, as will be gathered from the foregoing remarks, have long been accustomed to scenes of violence and bloodshed. They are simply slaves to the lust and rapacity of their ruler. It is for this reason that the holocaust reported to have been offered by King Theebau may perhaps have been a fact. Astrologers are an influential sect in this remote part of the world, and it is not improbable that so stupendous a sacrifice was instigated by them. No nation on earth, excepting the Hindoo, are so superstitious. They practice divination, they believe in witches, they wear talismans, and they use love philters. As fatalists they rival the Arab and the Turk. Their religion, that of Buddha, forbids the killing of any of the lower animals; perhaps it is on this account that they take revenge on their own species, and count man's life of little worth. For instance, if a person is accidentally killed by another, reparation is made by paying the price of his or her body, according to a nicely adjusted scale, which takes even the thousandth part of a dollar into account. I have heard of people being killed by inches, but never, until I went to Burmah, did I know that their lives were valued by mills. But in this strange land the life of a new-born male child is gauged at $2.50; that of a female child, $1.75. One would like to understand the moral principle which underlies the difference in these equations. A young boy is valued at $6.25; a girl at $4.37½. The price at which a young man is estimated is $18.75; a young woman, $20.62½. Upon what physical or psychical basis should there be this differentiation, amounting to $1.87½? The Burmese consciousness alone can tell. Though these are ridiculously low valuations, the greatest intrinsic worth is attached by this nation to its young women. The elephant, however, is valued at $50, or more than double the rate at which the charms of the most highly appraised human being are measured. But, in fact, the royal white elephant takes rank immediately after the royal family. The Cambodian king is actually styled the first cousin of the white elephant; and had Theebau died from his excesses, the Burmese, in the absence of all legitimate successors, might have taken a new departure, and allowed this noble and illustrious animal to ascend the blood-empurpled throne.

King Theebau does not appear to advantage when compared with his royal neighbors the King of Cambodia and the brilliant young potentate of Siam. These three peoples and countries are similar in many respects; the chief difference is in their rulers. A number of years ago, contrary to all Eastern tradition and etiquette, the monarchs of Siam and Cambodia vacated their respective thrones for a while, and traveled the one to Java and India, and the other to Pekin and Hong-Kong. Even so limited a view of the outside world as this, and amid nations not totally at variance with themselves in the general significance of their institutions, must have materially broadened the ideas of these semi-civilized monarchs. The only journey ever made by Theebau was the involuntary one to Madras, as a prisoner of the British Government.

Away from Mandalay I found the Burmese a simple-minded, indolent race, frank and courteous, fond of amusement, delighting in gay-colored apparel, friendly among themselves, and hospitable to strangers. But in the capital the tyrannous rapacity of the King and the unblushing venality of his officers created an influence which was but too sadly reflected in the bearing and deportment of the people. Throughout Burmah there were the strangest minglings of truth and error, sense and fatuity. For the past twenty years the country has been in a unique state of transition, and the conflict between old barbarism and new civilization has produced the effect of a rainbow illuminating chaos. Burmah, unlike Japan, has not yet become magnetized by Europe and America. Still, something has been effected, not only by English, French, and Italian merchants, but by the American missionary. A French protectorate has made Cambodia known to civilization and recognized by commerce. Under an English protectorate Burmah will speedily realize law and order where anarchy and panic have so long prevailed. Something like this is needed for the salvation of a nation stopped on its march to progress by the monstrous vagaries of a barbarian maddened with despotism and drink.

V.

THE EXILED EMPEROR.

" THE empire is dead—long live the republic!" Such is the exclamation which many democrats who saw no good in the form of government administered by Dom Pedro doubtless made when news came that he was dethroned. Yet if republicans can ever feel entirely justified in sympathizing profoundly with the political misfortunes of any discrowned sovereign, such justification may eminently be felt in the case of the recent monarch of Brazil. Born to a throne, he never prated of the right divine. Glorified by the nimbus of a crown, he put it on and off as a gentleman dons and doffs his hat. He used his scepter to free the enslaved. It became in his hands a divining rod by which he found out where evil flourished that he might charm it away if possible. He was more democratic, not only in manner, but in feeling, than many a self-made millionaire who fought his way from the gutter among the democracy of our own United States.

It is for these reasons, and because the change of Brazil from an empire to a republic has been accomplished with such astonishing celerity, that attention is almost equally riveted upon the dethroners and the dethroned. The people in this country do not cease to care what becomes of Dom Pedro because they care very much what becomes of the nation he no longer rules. The Brazilians have begun without bloodshed an experiment which with us was baptized in blood, and is now a century old. In fact, our interest is quickened in all the States of South and Central America, which, until recently, seemed so languid in political importance and so remote in commercial advantages. When we remember that the ex-Emperor is living thousands of miles from the capital where he seemed to reign in such affectionate security; that the action taken by the new congress which is soon to assemble at Rio Janeiro can not fail to be momentous; that the deliberations of the Pan-American Conference at Washington are full of significance; that the outlook of the Central American Federation is decidedly favorable; that the genius of progress still presides over the Nicaragua Canal; and that even the great intercontinental railway from Mexico to the Argentine Republic promises inception—the social and political questions that arise brim with more than ordinary importance and concern.

Out from among these complicated movements, the Brazilian phenomenon stands in startling picturesqueness. The Protean metamorphosis may be compared to an explosion without noise, an earthquake without shock, a cyclone without ruin. A dynasty has been dissolved as quietly as a pearl in vinegar. The depreciation of the national securities upon the stock exchanges of Europe and the United States has been only nominal. True, everybody in Brazil had been looking forward to a republic, but not until after Dom Pedro's death. There was no personal antagonism to the Emperor. Treason, disguised as a courtier, did not fawn around the steps of the throne the better to devise how best to level them. The ruler was respected and beloved by all classes. The merit of his character gave glory to his royal investiture. The kinghood of the man gave manhood to the king. This fact will connect his name imperishably with the history of Brazil and survive provisional manifestoes, a definite government named by the people, and the creation of a new constitution.

A few years ago I had the honor of several interviews with Dom Pedro, when he was at the height of his popularity and power. These interviews took place at his palace in Rio Janeiro and at his summer residence at Petropolis, and are described in detail in my volume Around and About South America, which has recently been published. My recollections of Petropolis are especially durable, because it has all the sylvan attractions of a summer capital, and because it was there that the Emperor made his dignified and pathetic reply when informed of his deposition. It is only twenty-five miles from Rio Janeiro, and is the most famous and best patronized of all the neighboring mountain resorts. There Dom Pedro and his household resided during the heats of summer, when the ghastly yellow fever threatened the metropolis, which has not yet been able to protect itself against the fatal visitant; thither the diplomatic corps and the native aristocracy followed in the suite of sovereignty, their own health and safety happily compatible with the requirements of court etiquette. There, too, flocked the families of wealthy Rio Janeiro merchants, the hillsides and valleys being speckled with cottages and hotels, men of business going and returning every day. The situation of Petropolis is romantic and beautiful. It stands amid a cluster of hills, twenty-seven hundred feet above the level of the sea. Though warm during the day, the nights are generally cool, and the air is always pure and wholesome. The broad streets are lined with trees, whose intermingling shadows repose the exacting eye should even verdure fatigue it. The houses are gayly painted and tastefully ornamented, and the grounds surrounding them are broken up with flowers which grow with all the profusion of nature and display all the delicate enhancements of art. Drives and walks, beautiful and irregular as veins of gold in quartz, radiate in all directions. The population is about ten thousand, among whom are many Germans. In fact, the general appearance of Petropolis is more German than Brazilian, the alleged reason being that forty or fifty years ago a colony of three thousand Teutons established themselves there. Altogether, it is a delightful sanitarium, where Rasselas might have been happy and Candide might have arrived at sounder conclusions respecting the philosophy of life.

Upon the day appointed by Dom Pedro for my reception, when I made my exit from the door of the railway station at Petropolis, there upon the sidewalk, with but a single attendant, stood the most democratic of monarchs, the Emperor of Brazil. So little apparent was the burden of a crown that his Majesty had the aspect of a commoner out for a stroll and halting at the station to see the new arrivals. His easy manner was marked by that entire absence of condescension which is thoughtlessly described as condescending, and was more like that of a civilian nodding to acquaintances than of a sovereign acknowledging the salutations of his subjects.

The imperial palace at Petropolis consists of a large two-story main building, with long, single-story wings, the whole made of brick and stucco, painted yellow and white, and of a style of architecture resembling that of a Florentine villa. To the most commonplace visitor it ought now to have a deeper interest of association than the villa of Napoleon III., pointed out to tourists at Vichy. It is surrounded by gardens and walks, in the turns and intricacies of which are found pleasant fountains and charming pavilions. The interior is plain but commodious. Not far distant was the residence of the princess imperial, a by no means imposing house, which, however, derived a beauty from the encircling mass of ever-blooming flowers. The Brazilian royalties generally took the air in barouches drawn by four mules, with postilions, and a single mounted orderly, and doubtless never dreamed the time would come when they should take it

15

at a day's notice in a steamer bound for Lisbon, or in lodgings engaged at a Continental hotel. They dreamed of it no more than I did, when, entering the palace, nothing was further from my thoughts than that the Provisional Government would inform the Emperor that his reign was over, and that he should reply, with scornful austerity: " I resolve to submit to the command of circumstances, to depart with my family for Europe to-morrow, leaving this beloved country which I have tried to give firm testimony of my affectionate love and my dedication during nearly half a century as chief of the state. I shall always have kindly remembrances of Brazil and hopes for its prosperity."

Everybody who has read much about Dom Pedro knows that his life at Petropolis, as elsewhere, was a very active one. It was not the restless and nervous activity of a Napoleon, who, whether he had Europe or Elba at his command, was bent upon making everything and everybody subservient to the caprices of his will. On the contrary, it was the well-directed energy of a highly cultivated and benevolent intellect, that desired less to rule than to have the benefit of his rule realized in the sphere over which it was exerted. His character had numerous facets. There was nothing of the uncut diamond about him. He was developed upon many sides, morally, mentally, and physically. He had seduously prepared himself for his social and political duties. What Lord Chesterfield was as a mere man of the world, Dom Pedro tried to make himself within the radius of a much more ex-

The Palace at Petropolis, where the Emperor was deposed.

tended and august influence. He neglected the body no more than the mind. He liked to take long drives and walks, and in his less mature days delighted in athletic exercises. He was compelled to relinquish these in great measure, more because of encroaching infirmities than because of that sort of decadence which is attributable to old age alone.

I am afraid that the popular impression in regard to the employments of royalties is founded, to a certain extent, upon the nursery tradition which sets forth that " the king was in his parlor counting out his money, the queen was in the kitchen eating bread and honey." Too many of us retain the convictions derived from early picture books, which represent the monarch, generally upon his throne, wearing a spiked crown (too painfully suggestive, however, of a crown of gilded thorns), his person covered with a gorgeous cloak spotted with dabs of ermine, and filling up the time between banquets by ordering recalcitrant courtiers to instant execution. We think of these conventional monarchs as going to bed still with their crowns on and their maces in their hands, much as they are represented in effigy on the tombs in Westminster Abbey. All these naïve ideas have to be fundamentally modified in regard to the ex-Emperor of Brazil. He was simply a gentleman with a scepter, a scholar in robes of state. He wielded the rod of empire as easily as a man in private life twirls a walking-stick. In 1876, when he landed in this city from Brazil, he arrived at his hotel wearing a linen duster and carrying a satchel. Only one other potentate landed as modestly —and that was Herbert Spencer.

All of us remember how Dom Pedro spent his time while here. He was out on the street at six in the morning, while his staff were still in bed, going everywhere, observing everything, and questioning everybody. He would have made a reporter of the first class had he not been a king. In perceiving, inquiring, and investigating, he ignored the divinity which is said to hedge the purple. In reaching the throne he had never had to use his elbows. He was more than willing to use them in getting at the real interests of the multitude. He was devoted to art and literature, to science and languages, and, to find time for this, he willingly dispensed with the cumbrous ceremonial and gorgeous festivities of a court. He speaks all the European languages fluently, and, at the time he received me at Petropolis, he was deep in the study of Sanskrit, though I am not warranted in saying that this was preparatory to a course of Theosophy, at present so universal a fad among cultivated persons. Dom Pedro studying Sanskrit at sixty was as interesting as Cato learning Greek at eighty, for Cato had certainly the more time of the two. The Emperor did not lose many minutes, for even while riding through the streets of Rio he generally sat bareheaded, his eyes fixed upon a book.

In fact, his mixture of intellectual and physical activity was remarkable. I have just read, in a Portuguese newspaper, an account of his life in Paris while on a visit to Europe for the restoration of his health. It is

amazing that an invalid should so sport with vitality, if
so profuse an expenditure of strength on legitimate objects may correctly be termed sport. Among scientists
whom he visited was the celebrated astronomer Camille
Flammarion. Attended by a suite of twenty persons,
Dom Pedro explored the astronomer's library and ob-
servatory, and examined his scientific collections and instruments. The gyrating dome contained a large equa-
torial telescope, an instrument of great precision, the
management of which, however, was entirely familiar to
the imperial visitor. The man who was really the fashion in the capital which has the reputation of making a
worship of frivolity was the man who is now ex-Emperor.
The only visitor who has since eclipsed him is our own
Edison, who created as much sensation among the republicans as Franklin, the first tamer of the lightning,
did among the court of which he was the cynosure. Dom
Pedro, living at the Grand Hotel, admitted a constant
stream of visitors, and ran as much danger of "making
himself common" as the President of the United States
during a hand-shaking at the White House. He talked
to all intelligently and modestly, reserving to himself the
right, conceded alone to kings and journalists, of asking
questions. His walk in life there was a tessellated pavement of business and pleasure. After frequenting scientific institutions, he indulged society with his presence
by attending balls. Whatever interested humanity appeared to come within his ken. Balzac called himself
the secretary of society, inasmuch as he professed to do

nothing but record his observations of it. Dom Pedro was also its secretary in a more restricted sense, for his observations, though not recorded for the public eye, were made with unflagging industry upon a vast range of material. He saw all the notable pictures, he was fond of meeting great artists. He did not forget the conservatory, he remembered the race-course, he was seen upon the exchange, and he applauded at the opera.

With but one exception, the reign of Dom Pedro is longer than that of any other living monarch. The accession of Queen Victoria preceded his by four years. It was during his reign, and through his exertions and influence, that Brazil grew steadily in power and standing. Few persons realize that that country is nearly as as large as Europe, larger than the United States was previous to the acquisition of Alaska. Of the South Amercan states it is the first, not only in size, but also in enlightenment and importance. It has vast resources. Its soil is fertile, its pastures are immense, its forests are gigantic, its store of minerals and precious stones is apparently exhaustless. The national finances are in a prosperous condition. Railways have been built, telegraph and cable lines have been extended in all directions, and all the large rivers have been made navigable. In these things, as well as in the abolition of slavery and the interests of free education throughout the empire, the hand of Dom Pedro has been felt. Procrastination in a good cause was not his vice. He can not be thought of as deliberately putting off till the last moment anything necessary—excepting death itself.

But, after all, the vital question is whether a republic in Brazil is likely to prove a success. We are not reassured on recalling the history of the neighboring republics which are peopled by a similar race. Nevertheless, had not Brazil been so nearly a republic in everything but name, it is doubtful whether the empire would have lasted so long. Governments, like religions, to be useful and abiding must be suited to the genius of the people who adopt them. Time alone can prove whether the sovereign power of representatives elected by the people is better for the Brazilians than a limited constitutional monarchy. As the talented and original Marie Bashkirtseff remarks in her suggestive diary that is now being so widely read : " No other form of government can be compared to the ideal republic ; but a republic is like ermine —the slightest blemish upon it renders it worthless."

Will the republic of Brazil attain this lofty standard ? Every worthy citizen of the United States should ardently hope so.

The military dictatorship, that constitutes the Provisional Government in Brazil, has the sympathy of the country, as is shown by the acceptance of the republic by all the provinces with very little hesitation, Bahia alone, tne conservative original capital, mildly protesting against the overthrow of monarchy.

The persistence of the new authorities in destroying all visible traces of the empire has shown the intensity of the republican animus. After the imperial coat-of-arms and flag were ordered down from all buildings, the streets rechristened which were named after the Emperor and his family, and the word " imperial" stricken from the common use, the Government ungenerously ordered that the " Dom Pedro II. Railway" be known hereafter as " The Central Railway of Brazil," and that the " Pedro II. Cóllege " should be " The National Institution of Instruction." In both of these the Emperor took great interest, and it will be impossible by the elimination of his name to suppress the identity of these and similar undertakings with his breadth of purpose.

The first move of the new Government in decreeing universal suffrage, instead of the educationally and pecuniarily limited suffrage of the old *régime*, and in dispensing extraordinary power for the state governments, has insured a broad popularity for its administration, even though the army sustaining the new Government has been largely increased. The words of Senator Paulo, ex-minister of two conservative cabinets, are illustrative of the general acceptance of the situation : " In the present circumstances, in view of the accomplished fact of the pacific revolution that proclaimed the republic, and taking into consideration the manner in which the population welcomed it and accompanies the logical developments of its consequences, the principal preoccupation of Brazilians is the necessity for maintaining order. . . . The Provisional Government will have our decided support so long as it keeps within the limits traced by the duty of securing the free manifestation of the national vote for the organization of the definite form of government. We believe that we express the opinion of all, or nearly all, the citizens, whatever be their political connections or affiliations with the parties to which they belonged."

The last move of the Fonseca Government, in postponing the first national election until next fall and in revoking the financial allowances made to Dom Pedro on the eve of his departure, are not calculated to inspire confidence in the intrinsic strength of the leaders, and the recent news of the death of the ex-Empress and her last words, " Poor Brazil! " condoling the misfortunes fallen upon the land of her constant thoughts, may cause an imperial reaction. But whatever the result, the world will always remember the wisdom and the kindheartedness of the Emperor whom Gladstone termed " the model ruler."

VI.

WHITE ELEPHANTS.

It is three hundred years since the Western World received the first extended account of the wonderful white elephant. This account came from an Englishman, named Fitch, (who must have encountered great difficulties in traveling through Burmah at that time), and may be found in Hakluyt's quaint and famous Collection of Nauigations, Traffiques, and Discoueries. This tells us that at that time the King of Burmah had four white elephants, which were very strange and rare. It also records that if any other king had one, the Burmese King would send for it, and would rather lose part of his kingdom than not get it. The chronicle further tells us that when any white elephant was taken to the king, all the merchants of the city were commanded to visit it, upon which occasion each of them presented it with half a ducat. As there were a great many merchants, this made a good round sum. At that time the white elephant stood in the king's house, and received great honor and service. Each of them had an apartment of its own, decorated with golden ornaments,

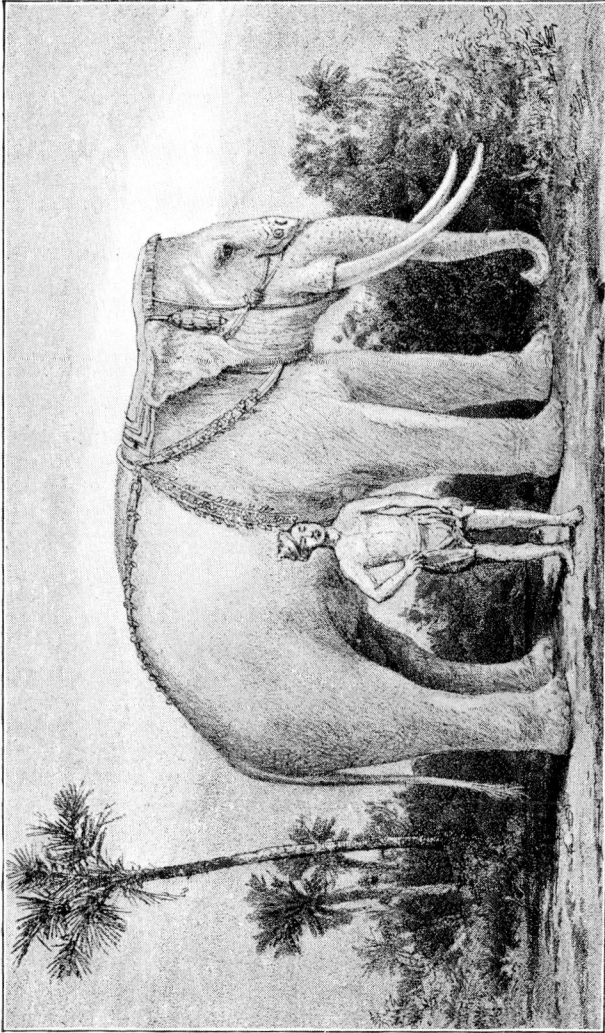

The Sacred White Elephant.

and ate its food from gold and silver vessels. Every day, when they went to the river to bathe, canopies of silk or cloth-of-gold were held over them, and drums, clarionets, or other instruments accompanied them. As they came out of the river each had a gentleman in waiting to wash its feet in a silver basin, an officer being appointed for that honor by the king. The black elephants were not so well treated. They were evidently regarded as the *canaille*, though some of them were very handsome and fully nine cubits, or thirteen feet and a half, high.

We next hear of the white elephant from Father San-germano, a Jesuit priest who labored in Burmah in the last quarter of the seventeenth century. He gives an account of the capture, transportation, and more than royal treatment of this fortunate variety. He tells us that, when caught in the forests of Pegu, it was bound with scarlet cords, and was waited on by the highest mandarins of the empire; that numerous servants were appointed to keep it clean, to serve it daily with the freshest herbs, and to provide it with everything that could add pleasure to the sense of existence. As the place where it was capt-ured was infested with mosquitoes, an exquisite silken net was made for its protection. To preserve it from other harm, mandarins and guards watched it day and night. No sooner had news of the capture spread abroad than immense multitudes of both sexes and every age and con-dition flocked to this central point. They came not only from the neighborhood, but from the most remote prov-inces. Finally, the king gave orders for the removal of the elephant to the capital. Immediately two boats of teak-wood were fastened together, and upon them was erected a superb pavilion, with a pyramidal roof similar to that which covered the royal palace. It was made impervious to both sun and rain, and draperies of gold-embroidered silk adorned it on every side. This splendid pavilion was towed up the river by three large and beautiful gilded vessels filled with rowers. The king and royal family sent frequently for tidings of the elephant's health, and forwarded rich presents in their name. To celebrate its arrival in the city a grand festival, which included music, dancing, and fire-works, was held for three days. The most costly offerings were contributed by all the mandarins in the kingdom, and one of these offerings consisted of a vase of gold weighing four hundred and eighty ounces. It is painful to be compelled to add, however, that all the gold and silver articles contributed eventually found their way into the royal treasury.

The particular animal here mentioned was as much honored at its demise as during its life. Being a female, its funeral was conducted with the same rites and ceremonies as those observed at the death of a queen. The body was burned upon a pile composed of sassafras, sandal, and other aromatic woods, the pyre being kindled with the aid of four immense gilded bellows blown at the corners. Three days after the ashes were gathered by the chief mandarins, enshrined in gilt urns, and buried in the royal cemetery. A superb pyramidal mausoleum, built of brick and richly painted and gilded, was subsequently raised over the tomb. If this elephant had been a male, it would have had the same obsequies as those used at the death of a sovereign.

The first introduction I ever had to a white elephant was apropos of my audience with the King of Burmah, at Mandalay, his capital, during my travels through Farther India. King Mounglon, the father of the notorious Theebau, was then upon the Burmese throne. The audience chamber was arranged somewhat theatrically. A green baize curtain descended from ceiling to floor. A few feet above the floor this curtain presented a proscenium-like opening, ten feet square, which brought into view a luxurious alcove. Within this alcove his Majesty was seated upon the floor, resting against a velvet cushion, with a cup, a betel-box, a carafe, a golden cuspidor, and a pair of silver-mounted binoculars within reach. He was short, stout, fifty - five, and pleasant, though crafty-looking. He was dressed in a white linen jacket and a silk cloth around the hips and legs. After staring at me a shockingly long while through his binoculars, he became interested to an unseemly extent in my age, my father's business, my design in traveling, and other personal matters. First, he made up his mind that I was a downright spy; then he concluded that I was a political adventurer; finally, it slowly dawned upon him that I was traveling simply for pleasure, and perhaps it was with the benevolent desire of enhancing that pleasure to the utmost that he offered me an unlimited number of wives (I did not inquire whose) on condition that I would

permanently settle there. Happily, the puritanical principles in which I had been educated enabled me to withstand the shock. St. Anthony could not have behaved
better in the circumstances than I did; and, besides, St.
Anthony's temptations merely existed in the abstract,
while mine were almost within grasp. Perhaps I ought
to add that I did not feel like entering the King's service
just at that time. While refusing all his kind offers
through an interpreter—and his Majesty offered me a
palace and a title, as well as a fortune, in addition to a
harem practically infinite—I succeeded in mollifying him
with the present of a handsome magnifying-glass, which
I had taken with me from Calcutta for the express purpose. This glass had a bright gilt rim and an ivory
handle. Though it passed into the King's hands then
and there, I have ever since seen through it everything
that is good in Burmah.

It was while the glow of this visit was fresh upon me
that I descended to the royal court-yard and there found,
in a sort of palace by itself, a specimen of the sacred
white elephant of which the world has heard so much
and seen so little. The creature was of medium size,
with whitish eyes. Its forehead, trunk, and ears were
spotted with white, and looked as though their natural
color had been removed by a vigorous application of
pumice-stone or sand-paper. The remainder of the body
was of the ordinary dark hue, so that it was impossible
for me to say that I was contemplating a white elephant
par excellence. The animal stood, I wish I could say, in

milk-white majesty; but, to tell the truth, its majesty was somewhat mouse-colored. It received me beneath a great embroidered canopy, a fetter on one of its forelegs being the only obvious symbol of captivity. This holy elephant had an intensely vicious look, so that I was fain to hope that behind a frowning providence it hid a smiling face. Umbrellas in gold and red occupied adjacent nooks in company with Roman-like fasces and silver-tipped spears and axes. The floor was networked with silver. Water jars and eating troughs, also of silver, were at hand to relieve its thirst and hunger. Fresh-cut grass and bananas were its staple diet, though it also delights in rice, sugar-cane, cocoanuts, cakes, and candies. The water it drinks is perfumed with flowers or tinctured with palm wine. The average daily food it consumes reaches the modest weight of two hundred pounds. Instead of its name, as we would place that of a valuable and favorite horse, a description of the animal, painted on a red tablet, was hung over one of the pillars of its stall. It ran as follows: " An elephant of beautiful color; hair, nails, and eyes are white. Perfection in form, with all signs of regularity of the high family. The color of the skin is that of the lotus. A descendant of the angels of the Brahmans. Acquired as property by the power and glory of the King for his service. Is equal to the crystal of the highest value. Is of the highest family of all in existence. A source of power of attraction of rain. It is as pure as the purest crystal of the highest value in the world."

The attendant priest told me that a baby white elephant, which had been captured in the northeastern part of British Burmah, had recently died in the capital, after a short residence there, and that the King had been "out of sorts" ever since. The precious infant had been nursed by twelve native women, especially selected for the honor, and for which service they were paid, my matter-of-fact informant added, fifty rupees, or twenty-five dollars, a month. But despite the caressing care of these improvised foster-mothers, their adolescent charge, as I have said, died, and the whole nation went into mourning, all occupations ceasing for several days, and the entire population shaving their heads.

As I stood contemplating the animal, it was not difficult for me to realize that, had it occupied its present position a century ago, gold chain nets and silver bells would have crowned its head, gay and richly embroidered cushions would have rested upon its back, while here and there would have gleamed strings of pearl and coin in miscellaneous decoration. Its tusks would have glittered with massive rings of gold, studded frequently with dazzling jewels. Each evening music would have allured it to sleep with the choicest melodies to Farther India known. Trumpets and drums and a large retinue would have preceded it to the bath, whither it would have been conducted with a large red umbrella held over it by some of the highest dignitaries. Young maidens would have strewed its path with rarest flowers, which it would have picked up at will, first smelling them by virtue of its passionate delight in perfumes, and then carrying them to its mouth, where they would have been apt to be sacrificed to the grosser sense of taste. Save for this occasional bath, however, all sacred elephants rarely leave their palace cells, except upon great feast days, when they always head the procession. Amid these happy conditions—provided they do not die of astonishment or succumb to indigestion—each might live to be a centenarian, rejoicing in a weight of two tons and a height of seven feet. And so profound is the Indo-Chinese belief in omens that an unusual grunt from this potentate is quite sufficient to interrupt the most important affairs and break the most solemn engagements. Consequently, the kingdom where one of these blonde and cyclopean beasts resides is thought to be rich and not liable to change, and the king is congratulated on being long-lived and invincible. Through his elephantine sympathies, he believes himself a partaker of the divine nature. In the Pali scriptures it is duly set forth that the form under which Buddha will descend to earth for the last time will be that of a beautiful young white elephant, open-jawed, with a head the color of cochineal, with tusks shining like silver, sparkling with gems, covered with a splendid netting of gold, perfect in organs and limbs, and majestic in appearance. From what I have said it is evident that in Farther India the more white elephants a state owns the more powerful it is supposed to be. The honors which the creature therefore enjoys are almost limitless.

The white elephant is often praised in language more
16

suggestive of Solomon's Song than anything else. Take, for instance, this passage : " His tusks are like long pearls; his ears like silver shields; his trunk like a comet's tail; his legs like the feet of the skies; his tread like the sound of thunder ; his looks full of meditation; his expression full of tenderness; his voice the voice of a mighty warrior," etc. This homage and superstition are reflected in the very titles and offices of the rulers and great men of Farther India. In ancient Burmah the king assumed the title " Lord of the Spotted Elephant." At the present day the King of Cambodia is styled " First Cousin of the White Elephant "; the Prime Minister of Siam, " General of the Elephants "; the Foreign Minister of Annam, " Mandarin of Elephants "; while the kings of Burmah and Siam both enjoy the still higher appellations, " Lord of the Celestial Elephant " and " Master of Many White Elephants." In Siam, too, everything bears the image of this lordly mammoth, to whose proportions, when in repose and when a pure albino, Mrs. Browning might have appropriately referred in that paradoxical line which speaks of " thunders of white silence." Like the lion in the Persian banner, the llama in the Peruvian, or the peacock in the Burmese, so the white elephant is emblazoned proudly in the banner of the Siamese. A badge of distinction is similarly created, and has become a coveted native decoration.

The constant companions of the pale proboscidian whose acquaintance I made, and, indeed, of all that variety, are white monkeys. Both the Burmese and the Siamese believe that evil spirits may be thus propitiated. As it is necessary to guard the white elephant from superhuman assault and influence, several white monkeys are generally kept in its stables. These monkeys are not reverenced for themselves, but for the protection—especially protection from sickness—which they are supposed to give to their gigantic comrade. They are generally large, ugly, long-tailed baboons, thickly covered with fur as white as that of the whitest rabbit. As a rule, they are in perfect health and veritable demons of mischief. Captured more frequently than the white elephant, they enjoy about the same privileges as it, having households and officers of their own, but they are always obliged to yield it the precedence. There is encouragement to Darwinians in the Siamese saying that the white monkey is a man and a brother—I might almost say a man and a Buddha. Upon that principle, civilized man, instead of being a little lower than the angels, is a little higher than the apes.

It will easily be believed that the capture of white elephants forms an important portion of Burmese and Siamese annals. In Siam only twenty-four were secured during all the thirteen hundred and fifty-two years that elapsed from A. D. 515 to A. D. 1867, covering the reigns of thirty-eight kings. This makes about one elephant for every cycle of fifty-six years. Of this number, several categories being made, eleven belong to the first. Even the great French naturalist Cuvier, in his celebrated Régne Animal, does not refer to such a phenomenon. The discoverer of a white elephant is rewarded with rank,

office, title, and estates, together with a purse of about
fifteen hundred dollars in gold—a large sum in white-ele-
phant regions. A very high and dignified position, to
which the fortunate capturer is frequently raised, is that
of " water-carrier to the white elephant." He is granted
land free from taxation, and as spacious as the area over
which the animal's trumpet cry can be heard. He and
his family, to the third generation, are exempted from
servitude.

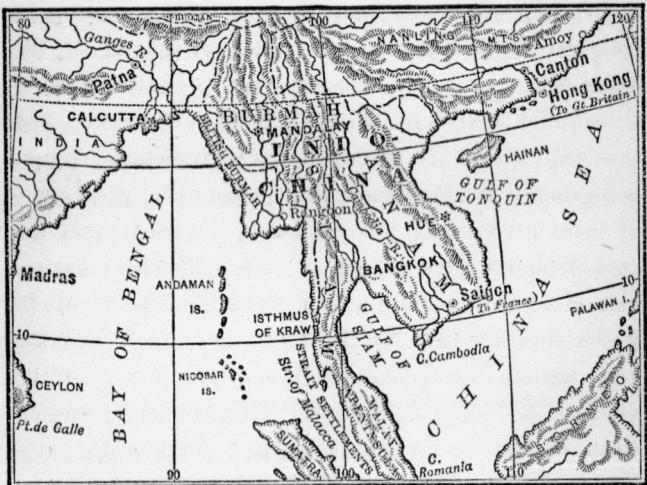

It should be borne in mind, however, that Siam is in
no exclusive sense *the* land of the white elephant, since
its habitat is the entire central portion of the great
peninsula of southeastern Asia, styled Farther India, or
Indo-China, and extending from the Bay of Bengal on
the west to the China Sea on the east. In fact, the

"white wonder" is seldom found within the strict boundaries of the Kingdom of Siam. Readers, and perhaps travelers, have been misled by the fact that the royal banner of that kingdom is a white elephant on a crimson field. But we do not look for unicorns and lions in Great Britain because they are emblazoned on her escutcheon, or for dragons in China for the reason that they are pictured on her flag.

White elephants have been the cause of many a war, and their possession is more an object of envy than the conquest of territory or the transitory glories of the battle field. Once the King of Siam possessed seven of these pallid pachyderms, and the King of Burmah asked that two should be given him, which modest request being denied, the Burmese invaded Siam with a great army of men, horses, and war elephants, marched upon the capital, and captured four of the hallowed monsters instead of the two originally demanded. The repute in which they are held by the court and people and the great anxiety there is to obtain them sometimes cause the destruction of much property. Thus, on one occasion, when a report was brought concerning the projected capture of a white elephant which had been discovered, and the transport of which to the capital over the cultivated country would destroy ten thousand baskets of rice, the king is said still to have ordered the hunt, exclaiming, "What signifies the destruction of ten thousand baskets of rice in comparison with the possession of a white elephant!"

Sir John Bowring, on the occasion of negotiating a treaty between England and Siam, some thirty-five years since, received many valuable presents from the king; but finally his Majesty placed in his hands a golden box, locked with a golden key, and containing, he informed him, a gift far more valuable than all the rest, and that was a few hairs of the white elephant! Most wonderful of all, however, is the compliment which one of the Siamese ambassadors, who some years ago visited the court of England, paid to her Majesty, the Queen. The ambassador, knowing that the royal lady had passed her life in an atmosphere of flattery of the most indiscriminating description, cast about for a metaphor that would express the sincerity of the Siamese mind and the grace of the Siamese court. He was not long in coming to a conclusion. Comparison with one of the unique beasts of which I am writing being considered a distinguished honor, the ambassador thus expressed himself: " One can not but be struck with the aspect of the august Queen of England, or fail to observe that she must be of pure descent from a race of goodly and warlike kings and rulers of the earth, in that her eyes, complexion, and, above all, her bearing, are those of a beautiful and majestic white elephant." If the Queen may be likened to a white elephant, it is not unreasonable to ask to what the rest of the royal family were likened by the Siamese ambassador?

Is the white elephant white, or only so by a figure of speech? To this question it is impossible to answer yes or no. The Siamese never speak of a white elephant, but of a *chang pouk* or strange-colored elephant. The hue varies from a pale yellowish or reddish brown to a rose. Buffon gives it as ash-gray. Judging from the specimens which I have seen, both at Mandalay and Bangkok, I should say it was generally a light gray, with spots or splashes of pink. The color of the true white elephant has that delicate shade which distinguishes the nose of a white horse. It has always a tinge of pink in it—that is to say, it is flesh-colored. The face, ears, front of trunk, breast, and feet, have a sort of pinkish mottled appearance, while the remainder of the body is of an ashen color. It should always be remembered that the term "white," as applied to elephants, must be received with qualification. In fact, the grains of salt must be numerous, for the white elephant is white only by contrast with those that are decidedly dark. A mulatto, for instance, is not absolutely white, but he is white compared with a full-blooded negro. The so-called white elephant is an occasional departure from the ordinary beast. As there are human albinos, so there are elephantine albinos. And there is a general resemblance of characteristics among all quadrupedal albinos.

It is not alone the amount of pink or flesh color that constitutes a white elephant. This animal must possess certain other peculiarities. Prominent among these are the color of the eyes, the redness of the mouth, and the white or light-colored nails. In this species also the hair, which is for the most part yellowish, is apt to be scanter

and shorter than in other elephants; hence the skin, with
its peculiar neutrality of tint shows more plainly. When
pink patches appear, they are due to the absence of dark
pigment in the epidermis—at least this is the explanation
of Prof. Flower, President of the Zoölogical Society of
London. The same theory accounts for the light-colored
hair. The iris is often red, sometimes pale yellow, sometimes pure white. When the latter is the case, the eyes
are white-rimmed. Sometimes, too, a pink iris is visible
in an eye that is rimmed with scarlet. I have heard it
said, also, that the pupil is occasionally a bright red,
though I have never seen this phenomenon. By the
dissection of white dogs, white owls, and white rabbits,
it has been discovered that the red color of their eyes is
caused by the absence of dark pigment. To put the case
in technical terms, the *pigmentum nigrum* of the choroid
coat, and also that portion of it which lies behind the
iris, and is called *uvea* by anatomists, is wanting. The
peculiar fairness of the skin and hair is said by those who
differ from Prof. Flower to be brought about by the
absence of a membrane called *rete mucosum*. An albino
elephant sees with difficulty in a strong light, but, on the
other hand, sees better in the dark than black elephants
do. I do not know that a scientific attempt has ever
been made to formulate the freaks of nature, so as to produce white elephants *ad libitum*. I am inclined to think,
however, that even the most intelligent Burmese or Siamese are not sufficiently conversant with Darwin's Variation of Animals and Plants under Domestication to

attempt much in this line. This variety of stirpiculture will probably be left to the future.

It is the general impression that white elephants are specifically different from others, but this is not the case. That they are distinguished from those species that have the ordinary color, by weakness of body, deficiency of instinct, or atrophy of mind, is abundantly refuted by facts. They are of ordinary size and shape, and specimens of both sexes are captured. When you possess an elephant whose color is that of a negro's palm, you possess a white elephant, the color not being necessarily hereditary, but caused by conditions so elusive that we are obliged, as a matter of convenience, to name the result a freak of nature. The hue is never a consequence of disease. Under identical conditions white elephants and black elephants are equally long-lived. Whatever in each species be the difference in shade, or whether the animal be found roaming in the forests of Laos or residing in royal state in the cities of Mandalay or Bangkok, I must not forget to say that the absolutely white elephant—white as pure snow is white—is never seen. As an ideal it may be imagined as enjoying a lonely paradise in some yet undiscovered jungle.

In Farther India there are occasionally to be found ordinary black or dark-gray elephants which are afflicted with a skin disease termed by dermatologists and zoölogists *leucoderma*. These elephants, at a distance, somewhat resemble the albinos, but a nearer inspection always shows that their eyes have neither a red, yellow, nor white iris; nor have their pinkish spots a sharp outline, but fade gradually into the surrounding hide. In these respects they strikingly differ from the albino variety. The greatest variation, however, is noticeable in their respective valuations, the genuine sacred white elephant in Burmah and Siam not being purchasable from anybody, by anybody, upon any terms; whereas the skin-diseased animal may be found without very arduous search, and may be readily purchased for five hundred rupees (two hundred and fifty dollars) or less. Notwithstanding this superlative distinction, ingenuous showmen have been known to so confuse these two varieties of elephants as even to exhibit the latter for the former.

I sincerely trust that these illustrations will make the matter plain, though I can not feel sure that they will do so until a genuine white elephant is seen here, or until my readers go to Burmah or Siam. But if it is difficult for the majority of persons to understand what constitutes a white elephant, it seems to be still more difficult for them to understand what constitutes a sacred elephant. That there may be no further confusion upon this point, I volunteer the following definition, which I think includes all the essential attributes, and none but those that are essential. Those peculiar qualities that make a white elephant what it is, make it at the same time a sacred elephant. It may be said that the sanctity and the whiteness (or what goes for whiteness) are correlative terms. Oriental religious credulity has always centered in albinos. When a Buddhist priest meets a white rooster, he salutes him—an honor he would not render to a prince. All animals that present white varieties—such as monkeys, mice, storks, sparrows, rats, robins, rabbits, and crows — have always been highly prized in the far East ; but the white elephant, being larger than all these put together, embodied more whiteness in one form, and was therefore reverenced by a people prepared for such a worship by the superstition of centuries. It was considered to be the temporary abode of a mighty Buddha. But the animal is now regarded as a deity, and receives divine honors only from the lower orders, who perform before it the *shiko* or obeisance indicating submission. The kings and the most intelligent nobles consider it an omen of good luck. It is, in fact, the " mascot " of Burmah and Siam, and to possess one is an honor that is envied. Even among the intelligent uppermost class this regard for the white elephant is carried to an extreme which resembles worship. The veneration paid has probably been somewhat exaggerated, but, in my opinion, the adoration lavished upon this pink personification of Buddha is as intense to-day as it was in earlier times. When one of these beasts is captured it is blest and baptized in presence of the king and nobility. Buddhist priests pour upon its forehead consecrated water from a great conch shell, and crown it with a pyramidal tiara of pure gold set with sparkling gems. Thus decorated, you would almost think it could say the catechism. Its Holiness is then knighted, and such high-sounding titles as " Gem of the Sky," " Glory of the Land," " Radiance of the World," and " Leveler of the Earth " are conferred upon it by the King, who thus exercises his prerogative as " Lord of the Celestial Elephant."

All authorities, from the English traveler Fitch, in 1586, to the Norwegian traveler Bock, in 1882, confirm the above statements. In 1617 Van Schouten, a Dutch traveler, wrote in his Journal of a Wonderful Voyage in the Indies that the Siamese " believe there is something divine in these animals, and adduce many proofs of it." Father Sangermano, the Jesuit missionary whom I have already mentioned, lived twenty-seven years in Burmah, and he says " white elephants are regarded as sacred by all the Indo-Chinese nations, save only the Annamese." Crawford, the chief of an embassy from the Governor-General of India to the court of Ava in 1826–'27, and who traveled and resided for over a year in Burmah, relates that just before he reached the capital a white elephant was captured, and the event was considered so joyous that the king issued an order to the tributaries and chiefs to ask pardon of the *Ka-dau*, or white elephant. Would not this be synonymous with regarding the *Ka-dau* as a deity? Father Brugière, in his Annales de la Foi, says : " Nothing can exceed the veneration of the Siamese for the white elephant." Sir John Bowring, who has written a very learned and interesting work on The People and Kingdom of Siam, tells us that " the white elephant is reverenced as a god " ; that " in the possession of the sacred creature the Siamese believe that they enjoy the presence of Buddha himself " ; and that " with the white elephant some vague notions of a vital Buddha are associated, and there can be no doubt that the marvelous sagacity of the creature has served to strengthen their religious prejudices. Siamese are known to whisper their secrets into an elephant's ear, and to ask a solution of their perplexities by some sign or movement. And most assuredly there is more sense and reason in the worship of an intelligent beast than in that of stocks and stones, the work of men's hands." Carl Bock, the latest traveler in Siam, says " a white elephant, however few the pale spots he may have, is revered throughout the length and breadth of the land."

After leaving Farther India I traveled extensively in Ceylon, and noticed that in the religious processions the place of honor was always accorded to an elephant of a light-slate color, but having a pinkish mottled head and trunk—or, in other words, to a white elephant. Such sacred beasts as these, I was informed by a Cinghalese Buddhist priest, were beyond price. He told me, moreover, that if I wished to see the most pure and perfect incarnate deities, I would find them in India-beyond-the-Ganges. He confided to me that the most sacred white elephant in all the world was then in Burmah, and that the fondest wish of his heart was to see it before he died.

The reader will doubtless now be quite prepared to believe that the Indo-Chinese nations would no more part with a white elephant for money than the United States would sell the dome of the Capitol or the right of religious liberty within our free domains. Some circus agents who a few years ago attempted to buy a white elephant from the King of Siam, at Bangkok, barely escaped with their lives, so intense was the popular indignation at the sacrilegious proposition. There is absolutely no possibility that even so reckless a sovereign as King Theebau of Burmah could, as was stated, have connived at the sale or exportation of a white elephant. His throne, and probably his life, would have fallen a sacrifice to the outraged adoration of the populace. This fact, and the facts that the Kings of Burmah and Siam seldom have more than one or two white elephants apiece during the same time, and are occasionally without any for five years together, cast additional improbability upon the stories of which we had such a surfeit in the newspapers. The kings of Burmah and Siam are too anxious to keep all the white elephants they can get, to part with one, at any price, and under any pretext. I would rather believe in the whiteness of a white lie and in the sacredness of perjury than in the combined whiteness and sacredness alleged of the elephant once added to what is rhetorically termed "the greatest show on earth." It would not have been more difficult to obtain King Theebau himself than one of his white elephants.

THE END.